# Bureaucrats, Policy Analysts, Statesmen: Who Leads?

# Bureaucrats, Policy Analysts, Statesmen: Who Leads?

*Edited by Robert A. Goldwin*

American Enterprise Institute for Public Policy Research
Washington, D.C.

**Library of Congress Cataloging in Publication Data**

Main entry under title:

Bureaucrats, policy analysts, statesmen.

(AEI studies ; 272)
    1.   United States—Politics and government—Addresses, essays,
lectures.  2.  Bureaucracy—Addresses, essays, lectures.  3.  Policy
sciences—Addresses, essays, lectures.  I.  Goldwin, Robert A., 1922-
   II.  Series: American Enterprise Institute for Public Policy Research. AEI
studies ; 272.
JK421.B87          320.973         80-10616
ISBN 0-8447-3375-X pbk.
ISBN 0-8447-3383-0

AEI Studies 272

*Printed in the United States of America*

*Dedicated to the memory of*
*Herbert J. Storing*

# CONTENTS

# PREFACE

It does not seem too much, from the citizen's point of view, to expect government to be efficient, modern, and responsive to the people. Citizens think it fair to ask that government records be straight, information accurate, services prompt and economical, and appointed officials hard-working and honest. In this computerized age, moreover, why should management of government not be up-to-date, scientific, and pioneering in the development of analytic techniques to anticipate problems and formulate policy? And finally, citizens rightly think that government ought to be capable of great leadership, in ordinary times as well as in times of crisis or war—leadership capable of guiding, improving, inspiring, uniting, and rallying the nation. In short, from the citizen's point of view, it is in no way unreasonable to call for government that is not just "as good as the people," but better—much better.

From the viewpoints of many who study government and politics, however, these "reasonable" demands generate frustrating difficulties. A government capable of fulfilling these expectations needs great numbers of dedicated bureaucrats, policy analysts, and elected officials; and tensions inevitably arise among them, partly because their natures are inherently different, mostly because the legitimate exercise of their separate functions brings them into rivalry for influence over policy making. The inevitable confusion of roles and struggle for leadership, and their consequences for the public interest, are the subject of this book. The question, ultimately, is whether modern democracy can generate the leadership to assure the survival of liberty in the world and nurture the hope, as Lincoln put it, "that all men everywhere could be free."

Most of the essays in this volume were originally presented at conferences held at the American Enterprise Institute and at the Public Affairs Conference Center of Kenyon College. The editor has sought to present the analyses and arguments of authoritative spokesmen of opposing views—as thoughtful, instructive, and responsible as we could find—but of such diversity that no reader could rationally agree with them all. The intention is to place the reader in the very center of a controversy that is stated powerfully and argued with conviction. The reader who cares at all about great political issues has no alternative but to think for himself and to come to his own conclusions.

The essay by Herbert Storing was not quite finished at the time of his sudden and untimely death. Acknowledgment is gratefully given to Walter Berns, Joseph Bessette, Ralph Lerner, Michael Zuckert, and especially Murray Dry and William Schambra for assistance in bringing it to the form in which it appears here. Margaret Seawell's editing was very helpful throughout the volume.

Acknowledgment is also due to Robert Horwitz and his Kenyon College colleagues for invaluable assistance in the development of this volume; it can be considered a joint venture of the American Enterprise Institute and the Public Affairs Conference Center of Kenyon College.

ROBERT A. GOLDWIN
AEI Resident Scholar

# 1

# Policy Science as Metaphysical Madness

*Edward C. Banfield*

*A statesman differs from a professor in a university; the latter has only the general view of society; the former, the statesman, has a number of circumstances to combine with those general ideas, and to take into his consideration. Circumstances are infinite, are infinitely combined, are variable and transient; he who does not take them into consideration is not erroneous, but stark mad— dat operam ut cum ratione insaniat—he is metaphysically mad.*

Edmund Burke, *Speech on
the Petition of the Unitarians*

In the past dozen years or so, policy-oriented social science research and analysis has become a growth industry in the United States. This has occurred in response to demand created by the spate of social welfare programs initiated by the Great Society and, for the most part, continued and expanded by the later administrations. Whereas in 1965 federal agencies spent about $235 million on applied social science research, in 1975 they spent almost $1 billion. Of the approximately $7.4 billion spent in these eleven years about two-thirds was under contract.[1] This brought into being several large independent research bodies, some quasi-public and others private, and it greatly increased the amount of university-based policy-oriented social research and the supply of social scientists. According to the 1970 census, the number of social scientists increased by 163 percent in the 1960s, an increase larger than that of any other major occupational

---

[1] The figures are from Clark C. Abt, "Toward the Benefit/Cost Evaluation of U.S. Government Social Research" (Cambridge, Mass.: Abt Associates, Inc., 1976). Abt's paper includes a table giving expenditures by department and by year. According to Laurence E. Lynn, Jr., in 1976 the federal government invested more than $1.8 billion in "social research and development." In Lynn, ed., *Knowledge and Policy: The Uncertain Connection* (Washington, D.C.: The National Research Council, 1978), p. 1.

group and nearly three times that of professional and technical workers as a whole.

The federal agencies' enthusiasm for policy-oriented research quickly communicated itself to the colleges and universities, which now take a lively interest in whatever may plausibly have the word "policy" attached to it.[2] Almost all the major universities have established schools to give graduate training in what is now called "policy science," and these have already turned out hundreds of Ph.D.'s. To be sure, not many of the graduates occupy high posts in government,[3] but it is reasonable to expect that within a decade or two they will dominate the upper echelons of the federal and state career services as well as those of some of the large cities.

The penetration of policy science into the executive branch has led to, or at any rate been paralleled by, a comparable penetration into the legislative branch. Congress now employs several thousand professionals, a significant and increasing proportion of whom are trained to do policy-related social science research or analysis. Some

---

[2] Lest this be thought an exaggeration, consider the following from a task-force report submitted to the president and the provost of the University of Pennsylvania by an associate dean of the Wharton School and published in the University's Almanac, January 15, 1974:

> Concern with issues of public policy pervades the University of Pennsylvania. Indeed, it is so pervasive that it is impossible to provide anything approaching a full account of the various educational and research programs relating to public policy. Virtually the entire curriculum of the Law School involves public policy. So does much of the research at that school. The Annenberg School of Communications, the School of Social Work, the Graduate School of Education and the Schools of Medicine and Veterinary Medicine deal with public policy issues also. Research at the Schools of Engineering and Applied Science has a substantial policy content. The City and Urban Engineering program, the National Center for Energy Management and Power and the Transportation Studies Center illustrate interests of this sort. Course offerings at both the undergraduate and the graduate levels and extracurricular science and society programs in engineering are similarly focused. The new graduate program in telecommunications engineering and spectrum management exemplifies engineering interest in public policy.
>
> City and Regional Planning is a policy-oriented program in the School of Fine Arts. The undergraduate Urban Studies Program is operated from the Provost's Office and involves faculty from several schools. The Wharton School, in addition to the many policy-related educational and research activities of the Social Science departments currently therein, has within it the Fels Center, the Rodney L. White Center for Financial Research, the Leonard Davis Institute of Health Economics, the Master of Public Administration program, the Industrial Research Unit, the Labor Relations Council, the Multinational Enterprise Unit, the Busch Center, and the Management and Behavioral Science Center.

[3] As long ago as 1970 the Civil Service Commission listed 563 "senior executive civil servants associated with program analysis." Arnold J. Meltsner, *Policy Analysis in the Bureaucracy* (Berkeley: University of California Press, 1976), p. 15.

of these are employed by individual members and others by committee staffs; most, however, are in one or another of several recently
established bodies: the Congressional Research Service (1970), the
Office of Technology Assessment (1972), the General Accounting
Office's division for program evaluation (1974), and the Congressional
Budget Office (1974). There is now serious talk of creating an additional body—an "Institute for Congress"—to be privately funded at
first and staffed by professionals "whose stature and ability would
earn the deference of the members."[4]

The scale and pace of these developments suggest that the
American governmental system may be undergoing profound change.
As "policy scientists" come to dominate the bureaucracy, not only
its decision-making procedures but its style and ethos will change.
In addition, those policy makers—"politicians," who are good at taking circumstances into account (they are "statesmen" only if they also
take a general view of society)—will find the bureaucracy more resistant than ever to control: policy science may make it a fourth
branch, almost independent of the others. If the analytical techniques
produced and propagated from the universities supersede the skills
of the politician and (on the rare but all-important occasions when
it is manifested) the wisdom of the statesman, the successful working
of the political system will be gravely jeopardized.

## The Methodology of Reform

The sudden growth of the policy sciences can be seen as a byproduct
of the civil rights movement and the War on Poverty. In the 1960s,
these brought hundreds of new governmental agencies into existence—all providing new job opportunities—and stirred the imagi-
nations of those who believed that government, if only it tried hard
enough, could cure the ills of society.

Actually there has long been a symbiotic relationship between
social science and social reform. In the 1880s, Frederick Winslow
Taylor spread the gospel of "scientific management" to businessmen
and, a little later, schools of business developed budgetary methods.
Late in the century, chairs in social science were established, and by
1920 all self-respecting universities had social science departments.
By then it was widely believed that government no less than business
should—and therefore could—be expertly run. (The city manager
movement got underway in 1914.) Naturally the social scientists in

---

[4] Alton Frye, "Congressional Politics and Policy Analysis: Bridging the Gap," *Policy Analysis*, vol. 2 (Spring 1976), p. 276.

the universities were looked to as a principal source of expertise for the organization and management of government, and thus of society generally.

At the beginning of the century, according to historian Barry D. Karl, there developed a methodology of social reform consisting of variations upon three basic steps: first a core group of specialists and influentials, coming together perhaps at a meeting of a professional group, would define a needed social reform or "problem"; then a conference would be called to broaden the coalition by bringing in journalists, philanthropists, and political leaders; and, finally, a survey would be made and a document produced "containing all the information and interpretation on which reasonable men, presumably in government, would base programs for reform."[5]

This was the method used in 1929 when President Herbert Hoover appointed his Research Committee on Social Trends, whose 1,200-page report, Karl tells us, established the principles that "social" behavior came within the purview of the national government, that "science" could do better at framing programs of reform than could legislators or citizens, and that "social welfare" was as fit a subject for national debate as, say, currency reform or the tariff.[6]

In the 1960s this method was used again and the principles were further extended in order to bring the social science establishment and the Great Society into mutually advantageous relations. This time the specialists and their allies acted through that most prestigious of professional associations, the National Academy of Sciences. A report issued under its aegis in 1968 defined the view that reasonable men should take toward the claims of the social scientists to be brought into the policy-forming process:

> The federal government confronts increasingly complex problems in foreign affairs, defense strategy and management, urban reconstruction, civil rights, economic growth and stability, public health, social welfare, and education and training. The decisions and actions taken by the President, the Congress, and the executive departments and agencies must be based on valid social and economic information and involve a high degree of judgment about human behavior. The knowledge and methods of the behavioral sciences, devoted as they are to an understanding of human behavior and social institutions, should be applied as effec-

---

[5] Barry D. Karl, "Presidential Planning and Social Science Research: Mr. Hoover's Experts," *Perspectives in American History*, vol. 3 (Cambridge, Mass.: Charles Warren Center for Studies in American History, Harvard University, 1969), p. 350.
[6] Ibid., p. 348.

tively as possible to the programs and policy processes of the federal government. Finally, the behavioral sciences, like the physical and biological sciences, require financial support from the federal government to continue to develop that knowledge and those methods that can lead to greater understanding of the basic processes of individual and group behavior.[7]

Although the report was remarkably adroit in the ambiguity, even confusion, of its wording, it succeeded in conveying the impression that social science had much to contribute to the making of sound policy. Its spirit, though not its letter, reflected the "social science utopianism" that, Karl says, was espoused by Hoover "to be a revolution against politics, committed to the rational, unemotional building of a new, scientific society."[8]

Policy science, in this perspective, appears as one in a long series of efforts by the Progressive Movement and its heirs to change the character of the American political system—to transfer power from the corrupt, the ignorant, and the self-serving to the virtuous, the educated, and the public-spirited; and to enhance the capacity of the executive to make and carry out internally consistent, comprehensive plans for implementing the public interest. These were the motives that inspired the Pendleton Act of 1881, establishing a civil service system based on the merit principle; the Budget and Accounting Act of 1921; the President's Committee on Administrative Management in 1937 and the two Hoover Commissions, in 1949 and 1955; and the Council of Economic Advisers in 1946. They were the motives that inspired proposals to replace politicians with experts in the legislatures and to do away with political parties.[9] When these proved utopian, lesser reforms were advocated that were steps in the same general direction: for example, changes in the organization and practices of Congress to make it an assembly of statesmen deliberating upon the great issues, instead of one of politicians arranging deals and running errands; and changes to require the political parties to "bring forth programs to which they commit themselves."[10]

Today's proponents of policy science are not as naively antipolitical as were the reformers of a generation or two ago; they do not

---

[7] National Academy of Sciences, *Government's Need for Knowledge and Information* (Washington, D.C., 1968).

[8] Karl, "Presidential Planning," p. 408.

[9] For example, Herbert Croly, *Progressive Democracy* (New York: The MacMillan Company, 1914).

[10] Evron M. Kirkpatrick, "Toward A More Responsible Two-Party System: Political Science, Policy Science, or Pseudo-Science?", *American Political Science Review*, vol. 65, no. 4 (December 1971), pp. 965–90.

think of themselves as engaged in a "revolution against politics." The old bias is still there, however; witness the intention to provide Congress with a staff of professionals who will earn the "deference" of members (why not just their respect?). Now and then distaste for politicians and their ways is made explicit, as, for example, when an economist, after finding that the structure of Congress falls "enormously short" of what is required for an "ideal" legislative process, takes some comfort in developments to which the Congressional Budget Act of 1974 may give rise: "With a well-trained, nonpartisan professional staff in both the budget committees and the Budget Office, it will be possible to reduce congressional reliance on the hearings process with its domination by special interests and the executive branch."[11]

## Social Science and Policy

The persistent efforts of reformers to do away with politics and to put social science and other expertise in its place are not to be accounted for by the existence of a body of knowledge about how to solve social problems. There was a time when social scientists thought that eventually they would find laws governing behavior, and most of them seem to have persuaded themselves that the discovery of such laws somehow would make for more democratic, or at least more effective, government. Pending the discovery of such laws, what social research had to offer was not solutions but problems. *Recent Social Trends*, for example, the monumental report of the committee appointed by President Hoover, attempted to establish the facts of social life in a way that would display to the public and its leaders the hitherto unappreciated extent and nature of social problems, but it offered no "solutions."[12]

Now, tens of thousands of Ph.D. dissertations later, there are few social science theories or findings that could be of much help to a policy maker—so few, indeed, that when the would-be writer of a "Handbook of Behavioral Sciences for Policy Making" went through the 600-odd pages of the "inventory of scientific findings" put together some years ago at great expense to the Ford Foundation, the

---

[11] Robert H. Haveman, "Policy Analysis and the Congress: An Economist's View," *Policy Analysis*, vol. 2, no. 2 (Spring 1976), pp. 242, 249. See also the lament of Howard F. Freeman (in his foreward to the work edited by Caro cited below in footnote 16): "Political pressures continue to result in expeditious [expediential?] decisions, which are then modified by counter-pressures." This, he thinks, "makes it difficult to be optimistic about the future for the world of social action."

[12] U.S. President's Research Committee on Social Trends, *Recent Social Trends* (New York: McGraw-Hill, 1933).

results were "insufficient for a short article, not to speak of a 'hand-book.' "[13]

To be sure, some social science theories did have an important influence on the development of the new government programs in the 1960s: those of Lloyd Ohlin and Richard Cloward on "opportunity structures" and those of Gary Becker on "human capital," for example, entered significantly into the conception of the Great Society's poverty program. Policy science, however, consists of the application of methods and techniques, not of substantive theories.

For several decades social scientists had been developing ways of assessing the relative importance of causal factors where several operated simultaneously. Further statistical advances occurred during World War II, when engineers, mathematicians, and statisticians were called upon by the military services to find answers to a wide range of very practical questions: What, for example, was the optimal search pattern for locating a pilot down at sea? Wartime experience produced a set of techniques—operations research—the usefulness of which in dealing with a certain class of problems was dramatically demonstrated many times. The class of problems was, however, a sharply restricted one: objectives had to be well defined, operations had to be describable by a mathematical model the parameters of which could be readily estimated from available data, and the current practices had to be ones leaving ample room for improvement.[14]

During the war there were also important developments in statistical inference, probability theory, and what is now called game theory. These developments were readily assimilated into economic theory along with the methods of operations research. Although economists were relative latecomers to the scene (the Rand Corporation had been in business for some time before it hired its first economist, Charles Hitch), they soon became the main force in the development and application of theories of decision making. The rapid concurrent development of computer technology encouraged

---

[13] Y. Dror, in Irving Louis Horowitz, ed., *The Use and Abuse of Social Science* (New Brunswick, N.J.: Transaction Books, distributed by E. P. Dutton, 1971), p. 127. The inventory was Bernard Berelson and Gary A. Steiner, eds., *Human Behavior, An Inventory of Scientific Findings* (New York: Harcourt, Brace & World, 1964). For a more recent compilation, this one financed by the National Institute of Mental Health Research "to demonstrate practical use of generalizations from social science to enhance social practice and policy formation," see Jack Rothman, *Action Principles from Social Science Research* (New York: Columbia University Press, 1974). One can get an idea of the usefulness of the "propositions" in this book from the following: "Success in community intervention varies directly with the sheer amount of practitioner activity or energy applied to role performance" (p. 71).

[14] See Robert Dorfman, "Operations Research," *American Economic Review*, vol. 50 (September 1960), p. 613.

the elaboration of highly abstract theory by making practicable the working out of computations that had previously been prohibitively time-consuming.

When in 1961 Robert McNamara became secretary of defense he brought Hitch and several of his Rand associates into the department, where they introduced the new techniques of formal policy analysis. President Johnson, impressed, it has been said, by McNamara's performance at cabinet meetings and also, one suspects, by the attention the Defense Department's "whiz kids" were receiving from the press, ordered all agencies of the executive branch to introduce "a very new and very revolutionary system" for program planning and analysis along the lines laid out by Defense. Most agencies found ways to avoid carrying out the order, which was soon rescinded by the Nixon administration. The idea of policy analysis, however, made an enduring impression on many bureau chiefs (perhaps because it offered them a means of establishing control over their subordinates) and also on those upper-echelon career civil servants—especially economists—whose exposure to the realities of the policy-making process had not yet made them complete cynics. Today most agencies have offices, headed in some instances by an assistant secretary, to clarify the agency's objectives, monitor its performance, and assess systematically the costs and benefits of alternative courses of action. It was partly in order to cope with the often highly technical reports produced by these analysts in the executive branch that Congress has added many analysts to its own staffs.

In the universities, economists, statisticians, political scientists, and others, excited by the new intellectual problems, challenged by opportunities to contribute to the solution of urgent social problems, and eager to share in the money and power of government, have hastened to develop policy science as an important field of graduate study. As one might expect, in most places the curricula developed for the prospective policy scientists consist largely of highly abstract methodological courses. Students without a considerable aptitude for mathematics cannot take these courses; that the student may have good practical judgment and a strong feeling for institutional realities will not overcome this fatal handicap. After all, the purpose of training in policy science is to improve upon practical judgment and to be able to substitute for it. It is not surprising, then, to find prospective students being told that they can hope to play an important part in public affairs if—but only if—they pass courses in formal analysis. (This presumably is what the Kennedy School of Government at Harvard means by a remarkable sentence in its *Official Register* for 1977–1978: "What the basic curriculum imparts to all individuals is essential to the effective functions of any individual who wishes to play an important role in the policy arena.") The curriculum of the Rand Graduate Institute is reasonably representative of that of most such schools: Microeconomics; Data Analysis and Statistics; Organizational Behavior and Analysis; Econometrics; Technology and Public Policy; The Scope of the Policy Sciences; The Adviser and Society.

## The Role of Policy Science

In the past fifteen years policy scientists have approached the policy-making process from several directions, none of which has brought them into intimate connection with it.

Perhaps the least successful role of the policy scientist has been that of proposer of new program ideas. Ideas that are really new are, of course, always hard to find, and, when one is found, it is very likely to prove either infeasible (perhaps because it requires skills or other resources that are not available) or politically unacceptable. At any rate, very few program innovations can be attributed to policy scientists. The Model Cities Program, for example, although preceded by the labors of two task forces, each abundantly supported by consultant specialists, turned out to be altogether different from what the planners had in mind.

Formal modeling—the development of sets of equations describing in quantitative terms the functional relationships in a system of behavior (for example, an economy)—is a mainstay of the policy scientist. There are models that purport to simulate the national economy, models that purport to simulate the impact of government policies on some part of the population (for example, of changes in welfare policies on welfare recipients), models that purport to simulate the effects of new transportation technology on regional growth, and so on. Unfortunately the models constructed by policy analysts are rarely operational. Unlike the operations researcher, whose problems characteristically involve technological relationships that are precisely measurable, the policy analyst typically models relationships that cannot be fully specified or exactly measured, and the results his equations yield—when they yield any at all—are therefore seldom of any help to the policy maker. "To the extent that it *could* answer questions," a model user complained, "they were questions that nobody was asking."[15]

---

[15] Gary D. Brewer, *Politicians, Bureaucrats and the Consultant* (New York: Basic Books, 1973), p. 165. See also W. Leontief's expressions of concern about the irrelevance, inadequacy, and "consistently indifferent performance in practical applications" of econometric models, in "Theoretical Assumptions and Non-observed Facts," *American Economic Review*, vol. 61 (March 1971), pp. 1–7.

Program evaluation—usually meaning the measurement of policy inputs and outputs with respect either to programs underway or to ones that are contemplated—has doubtless absorbed more time and money in the last decade than has all other policy research put together. The eruption in the 1960s of scores of new social programs, coinciding as it did with the vogue of policy research, led to serious, systematic efforts, often by "outside" research bodies, to measure the cost-effectiveness of the programs. Programs in health, manpower training, law enforcement, housing, and so on are now more or less routinely studied in the administering agencies or in independent bodies under contract to them and by the General Accounting Office (whose authority to make such studies was much extended by the Legislative Reorganization Act of 1970 and the Congressional Budget Act of 1974).

Generally speaking, these evaluations, especially those done by outside agencies, have shown the social programs to be ineffective, or at least far less effective than their proponents claimed. They have, however, had remarkably little effect on policy: one can think of no program that was terminated, or even very substantially revised, because of an evaluation by policy scientists. Findings that do not support "what everyone knows" or that run contrary to the interest of some politically important group (organized teachers, for example) are especially likely to be ignored. The testimony of Peter Rossi, the sociologist, is instructive:

> It is an article of faith among educators that the smaller the class per teacher, the greater the learning experience. Research on this question goes back to the very beginnings of empirical research in educational social science in the early 1920s. There has scarcely been a year since without several dissertations and theses on this topic, as well as larger researches by mature scholars—over 200 of them. . . . Results? *By and large, class size has no effect on learning by students, with the possible exception of the language arts.*
> What effect did all this have on policy? Virtually none. Almost every proposal for better education calls for reduced class size. Even researchers themselves have been apologetic, pointing out how they *might* have erred.[16]

The technical inadequacies of retrospective evaluation have caused policy scientists increasingly to call for experimentation. Economic reasoning, sophisticated analysis, sample surveys, and obser-

---

[16] Peter Rossi, "Evaluating Social Action Programs," in Francis G. Caro, ed., *Readings in Evaluation Research* (New York: Russel Sage, 1971), p. 278.

vational studies, a team of distinguished statisticians writes, will give some good "guesses . . . but we still will not know how things will work in practice until we try them *in practice*."[17] Policy scientists want to try out policies under conditions that are carefully controlled in order to measure the effects of a change in a specified variable (the teacher-pupil ratio, say) on the achievement of an objective (improved learning). Social experiments—"randomized controlled field trials"— are of course far more expensive than retrospective evaluations (six conducted thus far cost a total of $162 million, whereas the Westinghouse Corporation's evaluation of Headstart cost $585,000).[18] They are also difficult, sometimes impossible, to arrange, as the manipulations of the experimenters are often unacceptable to the subjects; and they are so time-consuming—usually covering several years— that the situation is almost sure to have changed materially before the results are in. No experiment, moreover, can yield reliable information about long-term effects, although these may often be the most important. That welfare recipients' willingness to work is not affected much by the introduction of a negative income tax, for example, tells nothing of the effects that such a tax might have on the work motivation of adults who were children in families with guaranteed incomes. Finally, it seems likely that policy may prove as immune to the results of experimentation as to those of evaluation. "After making a head-piece," de Jouvenal reminds us, "Don Quixote tested it by striking it with his sword. The headpiece shattered. He reassembled it, but this time did not strike it, for fear of again losing a possibly worthless helmet."[19]

Recently policy analysts have been turning their attention to "implementation"—the systematic analysis of what is involved in carrying out a course of action. A leading practitioner, Alain Enthoven, formulates the key questions as follows: "Will the people or organizations affected really respond as assumed? What incentives motivate them? Is the proposed course of action compatible with the institutions that must carry it out?"[20] To illustrate what is involved, Enthoven recalls that in 1967 he advised Secretary of Defense McNamara to approve a "thin veil" ABM defense system designed to protect ICBM silos. The Army, which for years had been planning

---

[17] John P. Gilbert, Richard J. Light, and Frederick Mosteller in Carl A. Bennett and Arthur A. Lumsdaine, eds., *Evaluation and Experiment: Some Critical Issues in Assessing Social Programs* (New York: Academic Press, 1975), p. 46.
[18] N. P. Roos, "Contrasting Social Experimentation with Retrospective Evaluation: A Health Care Perspective," *Public Policy*, vol. 23 (Spring 1975), p. 254.
[19] Bertrand de Jouvenal, *The Art of Conjecture* (New York: Basic Books, 1967), p. 103.
[20] Alain Enthoven in Richard Zeckhauser et al., eds., *Benefit-Cost and Policy Analysis: 1974* (Chicago: Aldine, 1975), p. 464.

a national ABM system to protect cities, persisted with its plan despite the secretary's order in favor of the "thin veil" system. "A deeper insight into how the Army would actually respond to the decision," Enthoven writes, "would probably have led to a different recommendation."[21] One wonders, however, how an analyst could have gained a deep enough insight into how the Army would respond to justify a different recommendation. Could a policy scientist have told the secretary that the Army would have its way no matter what he (the secretary) might decide? Dealing as it must with such extreme uncertainties, "implementation" appears to be a most unsuitable subject for policy science.

## Limitations of Techniques

Enough has been said of these principal tasks of the policy scientist to reveal sharp limitations on his techniques. Some of these are of such a nature that they cannot be eliminated or even much reduced by better theorizing or by further advances in computer technology. There can be no "scientific method" for developing new program ideas, for example. It will always be impossible to construct a formal model that will be of use to policy makers when, as is invariably the case with the "important" problems, one cannot identify all the crucial parameters or match them with adequate data. No one will ever find a technique for discovering the concrete implications of vague, contradictory, and fluctuating purposes. There is no logic by which one can pass from axiological principles to particular value judgments, and there can be no nonarbitrary way of finding the optimal terms of trade at the margin among government objectives when—as is always the case—they are not given to begin with. Finally there is no "objective" way of making correct probability judgments: some ways of making such judgments are surely better than others, but none can altogether exclude guesswork. Even if the policy scientist could know precisely what constitutes "good housing," "good schooling," and so on, he could not know (except in cases so obvious as not to need analysis) which policy alternative would yield the preferred set of consequences. In a world in which everything, including opinions as to what is preferable, is subject to rapid change, this limitation must be of enormous importance. Despite his claims to method and technique, the policy scientist must in all these matters make up his mind very much as the layman does and always has done.[22]

---

[21] Ibid., pp. 464–65.

[22] After noting that "there is almost no scientific knowledge concerning the long term effects of punishment on the amount of crime" and these effects may be the most

If to the inherent limitations on analytical techniques one adds the existential ones, policy science appears feebler still. Consider, for example, the practical difficulties in the way of getting reliable data on almost anything: for example, in 1960 and again in 1970 the Bureau of the Census failed to count one black male in ten; and in 1970 the Bureau, having concluded that its 1960 and 1950 data on housing conditions were highly inaccurate, then collected none at all.

There are practical difficulties, too—sometimes insuperable ones—in getting policy makers to take the work of the analyst seriously, and these are likely to exist even if the analyst's work *deserves* to be taken seriously. Some arise from the analyst's failure to speak a language that the policy maker understands. To be sure, many of those who have been trained in the techniques of policy science can adapt to a policy-making setting by subordinating "science" to common sense. A policy scientist who lacks this flexibility, however, is likely to find that he can communicate only with other policy scientists. The political executive, whether elected or appointed, and the law maker and his staff, although intelligent and well informed, do not know now and are not likely in the future to know enough statistics to interpret the analyst's reports; indeed, the method and mode of thought of the analyst are likely to strike the practical man as perverse, even ridiculous.

The widest gulf between the analyst and the policy maker is not one of communications, however. The more important fact is that what is of primary importance to the former is generally of little or no importance to the latter. Typically the agency head is chiefly concerned with maintaining and enhancing his organization, and therefore with things that may make a good impression on those (the White House, congressional committees, interest groups, media, and so on) who can help or hurt in this; the analyst's words will carry weight with him only when and insofar as they are useful in his day-to-day task of fending off the agency's enemies and bringing its friends into a closer embrace. The elected official's case is not essentially different: typically his main concern is in being reelected, and to spend time and effort on matters that do not promise to improve his position with his constituents by the time of the next election—six years hence at the most—is a luxury he rarely can afford. The conclusions ("hypotheses") of a study of the responses of a Senate

---

important, an analyst of the U.S. Department of Justice concludes: "For the foreseeable future, careful *a priori* reasoning, descriptive evidence on human nature and criminogenic processes, and common sense will rightfully remain the principal sources of evidence in the debate over criminal justice policy." Philip J. Cook, in U.S. Department of Justice, "Punishment and Crime," Working Paper, Economic Research Program, Office of Policy and Planning, August 1976, Opp-ERP 76-3, p. 54.

committee and of officials of the Food and Drug Administration to policy analysis are therefore not at all surprising: "Congress is almost totally impervious to systematic analysis, particularly in the short run."[23]

If the policy maker himself is impervious to policy analysis, its impact on *policy* may nevertheless be great. Indeed, the proliferation of policy science is making policy problems more numerous and complex. David Cohen and Janet Weiss show this in their review of the "torrent" of research done on schools and race since the *Brown v. Board of Education* decision. One study, they found, led to another that was more sophisticated, and then to still another, and so on. The quality of research improved as the process went on, but the outcome was usually not greater clarity about what to think or do, but, instead, a greater sense of complexity, a shifting in the terms of the problem, and more "mystification" in the interpretation of findings. "One thing is clear from this story," Cohen and Weiss conclude, "the more research on a social problem prospers, the harder it is for policy-makers and courts to get the sort of guidance they often want: clear recommendations about what to do, or at least clear alternatives." At its best, they say, social research "provides a reasonable sense of the various ways a problem can be understood and a reasonable account of how solutions might be approached."[24] Perhaps one is justified in concluding (as they do not) that it is easily possible to have too much of a good thing: that an analytical society may increase its problems while decreasing its ability to cope with them.

## The Effects of Policy Science

What has been said so far should relieve any reader who might have feared that the policy scientists are exercising undue influence. In fact, they have very little influence, certainly very little of a direct kind. What someone said of the decisions resulting in Medicare and Medicaid—that they were the result of negotiations between "Wilbur

[23] David Seidman, "The Politics of Policy Analysis," *Regulation*, vol. 1 (July/August 1977), p. 35. "The consensus seems to be," writes Carol H. Weiss, "that most research studies bounce off the policy process without making much of a dent on the course of events." She adds, however, that several studies "suggest that the major effect of research on policy may be the gradual sedimentation of insights, theories, concepts, and ways of looking at the world." See "Research for Policy's Sake: The Enlightenment Function of Social Research," *Policy Analysis*, vol. 3 (Fall 1977), pp. 532, 535.
[24] David K. Cohen and Janet A. Weiss, "Social Science and Social Policy: Schools and Race," in Carol H. Weiss, ed., *Using Social Research in Public Policy Making* (Lexington, Mass.: D.C. Heath and Company, 1977), pp. 67–83.

and Wilbur" (Congressman Wilbur Mills and Health, Education, and Welfare Secretary Wilbur Cohen) and were not directly related to any research—may doubtless be said of almost all the important decisions made with regard to foreign affairs, energy, welfare, and the rest. When still a Rand analyst, James R. Schlesinger gave "two cheers and a half" for policy analysis; it would, he said, "shake up many a stale mill pond." But he went on to assert—as he himself has recently demonstrated—that democratic policies would remain unchanged: "a combination of pie-in-the-sky and a-bird-in-the-hand."[25]

The political institutions handed down by the Founding Fathers have proved remarkably resistant to all efforts to make political life more rational. Perfectly aware that the great task of government is to give political leadership—to create and maintain conditions that foster the growth of a public opinion capable of intelligent discussion and of eventual agreement—the Founders were also perfectly aware that that task could never be fully accomplished. The nature of man, as they understood it, precluded the replacement of politics by reason. "Men," Hamilton warned in *Federalist*, No. 6, "are ambitious, vindictive, and rapacious." They were susceptible to some improvement but not to a great deal: certainly they could not, as the *philosophes* supposed, be brought to perfection. Struggle and conflict, however mutually disadvantageous, were ineradicable, and therefore the problem of the statesman was to find ways of containing them, not of eliminating them. In the system of checks and balances that they devised, the Founders responded to the political realities of their day (to the conflict between large states and small and the North and South particularly) and to what they knew would be the continuing fact of political struggle.

That the structure of the federal system has remained thus far sufficiently fragmented to ensure the supremacy of a more or less democratic politics may lead us to overlook or underestimate the importance of tendencies that have long been at work, that are now accelerating, and that have changed and will change further the essential character of our political system. Modern America, according to Robert E. Lane, has for some time been moving in the direction of becoming a "knowledgeable society"—that is, one in which, more

---

[25] James R. Schlesinger, "Systems Analysis and the Political Process," *Journal of Law and Economics*, vol. 11 (October 1968), p. 297. Formal analysis is itself sometimes a political weapon. In *Models in the Policy Process* (Russell Sage, 1976), p. 337, Martin Greenberger, Matthew A. Crenson, and Brian L. Crissey write: "the use of models to dramatize or publicize particular points of view is overshadowing their use for the enlightenment of policymakers." See also Howard Pack and Janet Rothenberg Pack, "Urban Land Use Models: The Determinants of Adoption and Use," *Policy Sciences*, vol. 8 (March 1977), pp. 79–101.

than in other societies, men inquire into the basis of their beliefs, are guided by objective standards of truth, devote considerable resources to getting and interpreting knowledge, and employ this knowledge to illuminate and perhaps modify their values and goals as well as to advance them. In support of this view, he notes, for example, that from 1940 to 1963 federal government expenditures for research and development increased from $74 million to $10 billion (he was writing in 1966; by 1976 the figure has risen to $22 billion); that from 1953 to 1963 expenditures for research and development by colleges and universities increased from $420 million to $1,700 million (in the following ten years they increased to $3,395 million); and that in the seven years from 1957 to 1964 the number of Ph.D's conferred annually increased from 1,634 to 2,320 in the life sciences (to 3,611 in 1975) and from 1,824 to 2,860 in the social sciences (to 11,040 in 1975).[26] That between 1965 and 1975 the production of social science Ph.D's increased fourfold while that of physical science Ph.D's decreased is surely a measure of the effect of the Great Society's social reform on a crucial component of "the knowledge industry."

If one assumes (as Lane does not) that the experience of going to college tends both to make one disaffected with social and political institutions and to give one a naive confidence in the possibility of improving them by some sort of social engineering, data on the increase in the number of college graduates are especially relevant: in 1900 there were 19 college graduates per 1,000 persons twenty-three years of age or older; in 1940, 81; in 1960, 182; and in 1976 (estimated), 259.[27] By 1985, about 20 percent of the employed population of the United States will have graduated from college—enough, surely, to affect profoundly the character of the electorate.

A principal consequence of growth in the direction of the knowledgeable society, Lane thinks, has been a shrinkage of the "political domain" (where decisions are determined by calculations of influence, power, and electoral advantage) relative to the "knowledge domain" (where they are determined by calculations of how to implement agreed-upon values rationally and efficiently). Politics, Lane acknowledges, will not cease to exist even in the most knowledgeable of societies, but as our society becomes more knowledgeable political criteria decline in relative importance, and professional, problem-oriented scientists come to have a larger say. This, of course, entails differences in the nature of policy itself. One such difference is in the very *consciousness* (Lane's emphasis) of a problem.

---

[26] Robert E. Lane, "The Decline of Politics and Ideology in a Knowledgeable Society," *American Sociological Review*, vol. 31 (October 1966), pp. 650, 653.
[27] *Statistical Abstracts*, 1976, Table 231.

> The man in the middle of a problem (sickness, poverty, waste and especially ignorance) often does not know that there is anything problematic about his state. He may accept his condition as embodying the costs of living. . . . Often it takes years of dedicated agitation to make people aware that they live in the midst of a problem.[28]

The curious thing about modern times, Lane remarks, is the degree to which the government undertakes to do what used to be done by the agitator; consciousness of a problem may in the knowledge society come *first* (his emphasis) to the scientific and governmental authorities. Knowledge thus "creates a pressure for policy change with a force all its own"; it "sets up a disequilibrium or pressure which requires compensating thought or action."[29]

Although he tries hard to avoid making value judgments (he is, after all, a social scientist writing for a professional journal), one gets the impression that Lane thinks our society improves by becoming more knowledgeable: now that scientific and governmental authorities take the lead in discovering and defining social problems, surely they will be brought to solution faster. That, it would seem, is the implication.

Lane's confidence in the scientific and governmental authorities is misplaced, however. This is evident from the examples he gives of "important findings" in the social sciences that have been produced by the scientific apparatus of the knowledgeable society: (1) The United States ranked sixteenth among nations in the rate of infant mortality in 1961 (ignoring the fact that the United States defines infant mortality more inclusively than do certain other countries). (2) It would cost about $10 billion a year to raise all the individuals and families now below a subsistence income to that level (the phrase "subsistence income" is, of course, meaningless; but even apart from that, the statement is misleading because measures to raise incomes of the "poor" to some acceptable level would inevitably attract many newcomers—how many depending upon the level set—into the "poor" category). (3) The reinforcing experience for convicted criminals while in jail results in high rates of recidivism (many other causes of recidivism are in fact more important). (4) Pollution of soil with arsenic pesticides causes cancer in school children (this taken

---

[28] Lane, "The Decline of Politics," p. 659. "The problem of liberal reform," Charles Frankel has written, "has become that of dramatizing for an increasingly comfortable people, the existence of problems that are not immediately visible and which it takes an exercise of imagination to recognize." *The Democratic Prospect* (New York: Harper and Row, 1962), p. 164.

[29] Lane, "The Decline of Politics," p. 662.

17

from Rachel Carson's *Silent Spring*). (5) The more an individual interacts with persons of another race or ethnic group the less likely he is to be prejudiced against them (could it be that persons who are not prejudiced are more likely to interact?).

Why are these "findings" important? Surely not because they constitute, or point to, "solutions" of policy problems. They are important as propaganda: by creating dissatisfaction they will lead to change. "Knowledge *and what is regarded as knowledge* [emphasis added]," Lane says, "is pressure without pressure groups. . . ." The influence of professionals and their associations, he acknowledges, is "not all good," but it is, he thinks, "generally responsive to the needs of society."[30]

One may well reach a contrary judgment: that professionals, because of their commitment to the ideal of rationality, are chronically given to finding fault with institutions ("bringing to public consciousness" new social problems) and, by virtue of their mastery of techniques of analysis, to discovering the almost infinite complexity and ambiguity of any problem. Like the social researchers of a generation or two ago, the policy scientist contributes problems, not solutions. But whereas in the past the problems appeared manageable to men of common sense and were understood to lie in the domain of the politician or statesman, now they have been shown to be too complicated for ordinary people to deal with, and they are, more and more, believed to lie in the domain of the policy scientist.

It is a dangerous delusion to think that the policy scientist can supplant successfully the politician or statesman. Social problems are at bottom political; they arise from differences of opinion and interest and, except in trivial instances, are difficulties to be coped with (ignored, got around, put up with, exorcised by the arts of rhetoric, etc.) rather than puzzles to be solved.[31] In coping with difficulties, formal analysis may sometimes be helpful, but it is not always so. (Would anyone maintain that in the Convention of 1787 the Founders would have reached a better result with the assistance of a staff of model builders?) Except in those rare instances where the problem is mainly a puzzle rather than a difficulty, the policy scientist is likely to exhibit a "trained incapacity" for performing what are the essential tasks of political leadership. These are, first, to find the terms on which ambitious, vindictive, and rapacious men will restrain one another, and, beyond that, to foster a public opinion that is reasonable about what can and cannot be done to make the society better. One

---

[30] Ibid.

[31] The distinction between difficulties and puzzles is elaborated by T. W. Weldon, *The Vocabulary of Politics* (Gretna, La.: Pelican, 1953).

cannot perform these tasks merely on the basis of general ideas or methods; one must have the ability, not taught in schools of policy science, of taking circumstances—infinite, variable, and transient—into consideration. What the political leader requires is not policy science but good judgment—or, better, the union of virtue and wisdom that the ancients called prudence.

# 2

# Statesmanship in a World of Particular Substantive Choices

*Mark H. Moore*

A statesmanlike decision is a rare event in our political system. For the most part, public choices emerge from the collision of urgent, well-positioned, particular interests. There is little in the substantive terms of debate, the process of deliberation, or actual policy choice that reflects the wisdom, virtue, and public-spiritedness that define a statesmanlike decision. More often, what governmental decision making displays is the rapaciousness of man. While we may be grateful that our system protects us from humanity's natural rapaciousness by pitting one scoundrel against another, the struggle between them provides no cause for celebration.

Occasionally, however, this collision of specific interests yields a much different result. A choice is made that seems to exceed the possibilities of the situation: a broader set of concerns is addressed, a longer time frame established, and a more subtle understanding of the world shown than there appeared any reason to expect. The choice made not only reflects this broad understanding of what is at stake, but also reveals a compelling discriminating judgment about which social interests should be given greatest weight among all those that are in competition. In such an event, there is cause for celebration. Not only do we benefit from the wisdom and virtue of the choice itself, but we see in it great possibilities for the future. We are instructed (or reminded) of the interests and concerns that are central to our society; we discover that people can, on occasion, be more than merely rapacious; and we find that the process of governing can produce triumphs as well as ward off disasters. In short, we realize that it is possible for a public choice to express our most highly prized civic virtues.

My hunch is that our society needs a few such triumphs each year to insure the commitment of its citizens. It is possible, of course, that the necessary commitment could survive without annual demonstrations of the potential for statesmanship. The determined optimism of liberals (who insist that every public choice should celebrate public virtue) and the equally relentless pessimism of the conservatives (who assume that checking rapaciousness with rapaciousness is the best that can be managed in an imperfect world) might shield both groups from any great disappointment with the actual performance of the state apparatus. More often, though, I think that both groups *do* need evidence of wisdom and virtue in public choices to sustain their commitment. The liberals need a few successes to rekindle their faith. And the conservatives, though they might never admit it, need a little something to celebrate. Without statesmanship, some of the glue that binds both conservatives and liberals to the state will be lost—and with it, not only the state's ability to govern effectively, but also some of the gratifications of being a citizen.

If we need occasional acts of statesmanship to sustain the republic, then we ought to be concerned about the factors that make such acts more or less likely. We understand, of course, that statesmen are necessarily rare. Wisdom and virtue individually are never in large supply; in combination, they are rarer still; and for the combination to appear in men and women who are attracted to and can survive the grueling processes of government is unusual indeed. The dearth of statesmen, however, does not necessarily mean a dearth of statesmanship. If our political processes hurl near-statesmen together and extract from them a choice that would have been beyond the capability of any one of them, then statesmanship can occur without an individual statesman. So, it is some mix of the qualities of people serving in the government and the processes that bring those people together that will determine the frequency of acts of statesmanship.

My colleague, Professor Banfield, sees statesmanship as seriously threatened. In his view, the growth of social science knowledge, the elaboration of its methods, the sheer increase in the number of social scientists, and the increased reliance of government on their advice pose a major threat to the prospects for statesmanship. Part of the threat lies in the allure that the apparently scientific methods of social science might have for conscientious public officials who confront difficult substantive choices and want to make them responsibly. Professor Banfield worries that these techniques will replace the judgment and wisdom of the statesman. Furthermore, he fears that, as the institution of social science grows, the ethos and style of politics will shift in a direction that limits the potential for effective governance. If both the consciousness of our officials and the processes in

21

which they confront one another become impoverished by the influence of social science, then the prospects of statesmanship will be reduced and one of the glories of public life eliminated.

It seems to me that there is a fundamental misunderstanding of this perceived threat. Professor Banfield fails to discriminate between a choice that is informed by the findings and methods of social science and one that is completely structured and driven by those methods. He sees social science as having limited capabilities and extravagant pretensions which together comprise a threat to wise and virtuous policy choice, and the guesswork, common sense, and judgment of experienced citizens and officials as the much preferable alternative. I agree that common sense and judgment are crucial starting and ending points in making choices about complex situations. But I also believe that common sense can be enlarged and tutored by findings and concepts from the social sciences. In fact, my view is that the intelligent use of the concepts and habits of thought one develops in studying social science could not only lend more discipline and structure to ultimate choices, but could also allow personal creativity and judgment to play a more effective role. The problem is finding public officials who are endowed with wisdom and virtue *and* capable of utilizing social science—who can use their own training in social science to inform their choices and also avail themselves of the products of social science research done by others. Since developing such people is the avowed purpose of my institution, the Kennedy School of Government at Harvard, I count myself as part of the solution to the problem Professor Banfield identifies, not as part of the problem, as he would have it.

## The Consciousness of Statesmen

It is by now a truism that the range and intrusiveness of governmental action seem to grow daily. We often attribute this growth to the internal imperatives of government institutions themselves. I suspect, however, that the impetus comes not only from the internal requirements of legislatures, political executives, and bureaucracies, but from strident demands for governmental action by institutions and individuals outside the government. Some of these external demands are traditional: private groups have always lobbied for exclusive benefits from the government. But increasingly the external demands are of a different character: government is asked to produce benefits distributed on a vaster and more equal scale. The benefits either protect or enlarge areas of individual opportunity and privilege which suddenly are considered fundamental to a satisfactory human existence. We seem to be trying either to express new ideas about the rights, privileges, and opportunities of being a citizen, or to protect what we thought Americans once had in a less technological society.

For whatever reason, the public agenda is loaded with complicated choices about specific substantive issues. If this is the environment in which would-be statesmen have to operate, some relevant questions are: How would we like them to respond to this vast substantive agenda? What should they see as being at stake in these choices? How should they make up their minds about what the public interest requires? What perspectives should they bring to bear? And what part can social science findings or formal analytic reasoning play in these decisions?

Perhaps the most important thing for a public official to notice as he confronts a stream of specific issues is that some of the most crucial effects of his choices are likely to fall outside the areas in which he is working. When he decides how long to carry on unemployment compensation benefits, or how aggressively to search for husbands who abandon families and leave them in poverty, or even whether to expand services to the handicapped population, his decisions are likely to have important cumulative effects on the fundamental institutions of the society. Every policy choice he makes accords with some concept of the future role of the state. His decision may affect the distribution of power and responsibility among levels of government; or it may strengthen or erode the power of private or intermediate institutions in the society. Since these institutional arrangements circumscribe future prospects for social action as well as the current circumstances of individual lives, even small and remote effects on them are highly significant.

We tend to assume that the choices that shape the future of our *institutions* will be made explicitly; we seldom think of them as having any relation to the narrow substantive decisions of day-to-day politics. Similarly, we assume that such major choices are the exclusive province of statesmen. When crucial institutional issues arise, we believe, statesmen and statesmanship will come to the fore. The problem with this view is that there does not appear to be even a forum for intelligent discussion of the design and development of our major institutional arrangements, much less an opportunity to direct their evolution in a deliberate, sustained way. Instead, changes in our institutions come as the cumulative effects of smaller substantive decisions.

In a world organized to consider and decide a constant stream of specific issues, perhaps the only way for statesmanlike concerns about institutions to emerge is in these very day-to-day choices. If this is true, then it is to the people who make these choices that we must look for our statesmen. This means that our statesmen also must have some of the specialized knowledge of substantive experts. It is the need for the combination of these different capabilities in the same person that constitutes the new and distinctive challenge to statesmanship.

It should be clear that the ability to see the long-run institutional implications of individual substantive decisions requires a perspective broader than that supplied by social science knowledge or formal analytic reasoning. It must arise from significant personal experience, knowledge of history and political philosophy, and a personal concept of a political and social structure which allows (and, ideally, encourages) dignified human lives.

Although it is important that public officials have some awareness of the long-run institutional effects of their choices, it is also important that they foresee the more limited substantive effects. We want them to be able to anticipate the impact of a large-scale expansion of methadone maintenance programs on the size and shape of the heroin problem. We want them to be able to judge how efforts to control handguns will affect the level of violent crime. It is in this area—estimating the likely consequences of alternative policy actions and choosing optimal policies—that social science findings and formal analytic reasoning might be expected to help statesmanlike public officials.

In fact, social scientists argue that their findings and methods are not only useful but *essential* for responsible public choices. Judging the impact of a given choice on the many lives it will affect requires tracing possible consequences of alternative actions through elaborate causal chains. The *empirical* methods of the social sciences are designed to determine which causal mechanisms will operate in a particular set of circumstances, and (occasionally) with what force. The *analytic* methods of operations research are designed to help trace the results of complicated chains of causation, and to make an optimal choice from among a bewildering variety of possible actions. Hence, without social science findings and formal analytic reasoning, it is impossible to see what the consequences of various choices would be, or to defend the reasoning that led to a given choice. In other words, social science can provide an accurate model of the way the relevant piece of the world operates—essential if one is to make a responsible choice.

To any conscientious decision maker or policy designer, such an argument carries a great deal of weight. It does seem wrong to decide a matter of great importance to individual citizens on the basis of uncertain knowledge of the consequences or illogical reasoning. Where important things are at stake, we ought to be willing to take the time to order our thinking and gather the relevant evidence.

The flaws in this argument become apparent only when one tries to put it into practice. Then the insufficiency of social science findings and formal analytic reasoning for structuring and informing complex public choices becomes all too evident. There are at least two problems for social science's role in policy choice—one quite fundamental, the other less fundamental but still likely to be troubling for the foreseeable future.

The fundamental problem is that few crucial components of any policy calculation are necessarily ambiguously derived. An explicit policy choice always involves both a set of objectives (or a set of valued attributes of the world that are likely to be affected by policy choices) and a set of policy options. If social science helps at all, it helps us to estimate the effects of various policy choices on our objectives, or to make a complex calculation of which alternative is better, given a set of values attached to the different objectives. The problem is that neither social science nor formal analytic reasoning tells us which attributes of the world should be considered objectives, or which options are available for consideration. These are likely to be suggested partly by the particular circumstances of a given choice, partly by the ability of the decision maker to see the complexity of the empirical world in which he is about to intervene, and partly by the decision maker's openness, imagination, and ingenuity. Thus, crucial parts of the definition of a decision problem cannot be deduced either from analytic principles or from well-established generalizations about the world. They come instead from the decision maker's sense of what is at stake and what actions are possible—that is, from his knowledge of the particular circumstances of his choice.

A less fundamental but equally vexing problem for the role of social science in policy choice is that the current stock of empirical knowledge, formal modeling procedures, and optimizing algorithms is not sufficient to capture the complexity the decision maker faces as he confronts a particular choice. For each decision, he confronts a slightly different world, comprising a great many variables interacting in complex relationships. To some extent, this complexity argues a need for formal analytic methods, since they can be helpful in organizing reasoning. In fact, however, when a policy maker tries to make a rigorous optimizing calculation about a situation, he finds that he lacks the empirical knowledge necessary to validate an analytic model of the particular world he is dealing with. Moreover, he is forced to make many limiting assumptions about the shape of that world in order to compute an optimal solution.

If a decision maker is not aware of these limitations of social science as he structures and resolves policy choices, there is a grave risk that his view of those choices will be distorted. First, if his commitment to a "scientific" approach causes him to focus on developing powerful empirical generalizations, lifelike computer simulations, or sophisticated optimizing calculations, he may not give enough creative thought to his objectives or to exploring the range of possible means to achieve them. Without a clear awareness of the goals of a potential course of action, and the various ways these goals might be pursued, no amount of scientific rigor in his calculations can produce an intelligent choice.

Second, as complex as the calculations in a policy design problem may be, they necessarily rest on a drastic simplification of the actual world. It is difficult enough to draw rigorous conclusions from very simple ideas about the world: we are decades away from being able to make rigorous calculations about complex ideas of the world.

Third, the intrusion of sophisticated social science into the structuring and resolution of a policy choice may mean that the whole debate will be carried out in an arcane language, accessible only to a few highly trained people. This obviously limits the opportunities for democratic deliberation. It is also likely to limit the chance for the social scientists involved to find out the limitations of their conceptions of the problem.

Fourth, although nothing in the logic of social science requires it, something in the sociology or psychology of *doing* social science tends to make those who do it overly confident, even arrogant. Many of them seem to believe they guard the world of truth against a stupid, crude, and uncaring practical world. Much of their training and their institutional surroundings encourage them to think this way.

For all these reasons, an orientation toward social science not only fails to guarantee decision makers the best possible policy choices, but it could lead would-be statesmen astray. In this conclusion I agree with Professor Banfield. The crucial question is: What is the alternative to social science and formal analytics in reasoning about complex substantive policy choices? Is it true that without social science, political decision making is mere intuition, guesswork, and judgment?

I am not convinced that this is the case. My own view is a simple one: Within the world of policy decisions that depend ultimately on judgment, experience, intuition, and guesses, decisions nonetheless differ in terms of how carefully and completely they are structured, how well informed they are, and how systematically alternatives have been considered. Careful structure, adequate information, and systematic calculation can be of great value so long as the price is not a radically simplified or abstracted view of the world.

I have described my hesitation about social science and formalism; I have not yet indicated my misgivings about untutored and unstructured intuition. The idea that a politician's intuition is the only tool he needs for handling complex choices seems to me little more than romanticism. Many intuitive decisions in fact reflect a simple-mindedness that may be as dangerous as the pretentious reductionism of the social sciences. A choice directed by untutored intuition often is extremely truncated: a small range of objectives is identified, a limited number of alternatives considered, and an evaluation made on the basis of shockingly inadequate empirical evidence and little rigorous thought. That this truncated form of the decision problem is cast in terms familiar to all gives it only a slight advantage over the social scientist's equally limited but more obscurely expressed formulation.

The alternative to both simple-minded intuition and simple-minded formalism is for the decision maker to define and analyze each problem in its own particular form. He may begin with a fairly simple conception, but as he proceeds with his evaluation, the terms of the calculation will grow: more objectives will be added as he perceives new potential effects of the policy alternatives he is considering; new alternatives will be generated as he becomes familiar with current practice in the area, historical experience, and perhaps the policies of other governments or cultures; and the definition of the problem may change as he breaks up general contributing factors into sets of specific causes. As the complexity of the problem thus emerges, three important things will happen. First, the decision maker's scope for action increases, giving him greater potential for inventing and combining alternative actions. Second, some means of ordering relationships and variables becomes essential if he is to use the organized structure of the problem to point toward solutions. This ordering must be systematic, but it need not be stated mathematically. Third, the structured but complex conception of the problem allows the decision maker to bring in all kinds of information about both the sizes of various components of the problem and the relationships among various factors, and it indicates areas where information is missing or uncertain. All this brings the decision maker closer to the particular circumstances with which he is dealing and provides room for creativity, rather than leading a decision maker into the structure of a stark, formal model with little room for ingenuity or insight.

The second and third steps in the process can be facilitated if the policy maker is sufficiently well trained in social science methods to use those methods to organize his ideas about relationships and draw on available information about magnitudes. But the value of the methods is as metaphors and qualitative guides, not as means of obtaining a simple quantitative solution to the problem. The methods allow the decision maker to reason more effectively about events in the real world. Understanding them also can make him a more effective consumer of the works of other social scientists, in that he is equipped to avoid being either over- or underimpressed with their careful observations and elaborate calculations. But this is a small benefit, I suspect, compared to his increased capability to reason clearly about complex choices.

Thus, training in formal empirical and analytic methods can be of great value to the would-be statesman confronted with complex substantive choices. There are real limitations to these methods, and some dangers in relying on them too heavily, but there are also substantial potential benefits. Combined with judgment and experience, the methods of social science can sustain a fairly comprehensive and probing exploration of the piece of the empirical world relevant to a particular problem. That exploration may suggest new approaches, or it may suggest different evaluations of traditional approaches. The calculation that informs the ultimate choice cannot be fully "scientific," but it will be relatively informed, careful, and imaginative—which is about as much as we can ask of decision makers. In a few cases, systematic but unscientific calculation may even become the crucial ingredient for a statesmanlike choice.

## Social Science: A Dangerous New Estate?

Beyond the disturbing prospect that individual officials might be misled by the promise of scientific solutions for difficult problems, Professor Banfield sees an additional threat: the sheer weight and momentum of the institution of social science. Representatives and officials might simply be unable to hold off the hordes of social scientists now skulking, but soon striding, in the corridors of government.

In Banfield's view, such a shift in the style and ethos of government from a political system composed of competing interests mediated by a variety of restraining structures to a technical debate among academic social scientists holds many terrors. First, for all the reasons noted above, the substantive aspects of the political debate would become impoverished in such a situation. Important interests either would be strategically disguised or would go unnoticed. Knowledge about causal relationships in the real world would be lost because that knowledge is found not in the results of a statistical analysis, but in the experience of people who have worked in the various substantive areas. Second, because the terms of the policy debate would become arcane, power in political decisions would shift from people with real interests, knowledge, and experience to people with relatively little experience but substantial academic training. This not only would further impoverish the debate, it also would deny most citizens any opportunity to participate. Governmental choices would cease to be expressions of a communal process of deliberation: they would become as empty and alienating as arbitrary orders from an incompetent superior. Third, partly because social scientists are motivated to discover and document new conditions in the society that require action, and partly because social scientists are *always* able to find flaws in previously adopted solutions to problems, the number (and difficulty) of problems to be resolved by government would grow astronomically. As a result, government would become a source of frustration for those who participate, a symbol of incompetence for those (increasingly few) who merely look on, and an arrogant, clumsy monster for those whose expectations and lives are buffeted by its starts, stops, and shifts.

Clearly this is a recipe for ineffective governance. If such a government were plainly imminent, and if the growth of the social science establishment were a major factor pushing in this direction, there would be not only occasion for handwringing but also, perhaps, a strong argument for braking the momentum of this emergent estate. Professor Banfield does not, however, make a convincing case for this threat to our political system. His paper fails to establish conclusively even that the influence of social science is growing. He does not consider the possibility that the role and contribution of social science could develop in a different direction from the one he predicts. Further, his argument does not preclude the possibility that the growth of social science is not an independent factor pushing government in the direction he abhors, but merely an intermediate result of much more fundamental processes.

Consider, first, the relatively simple issue of whether or not social science is becoming more influential in policy deliberations. Professor Banfield begins his paper with observations and statistics designed to give the impression that a juggernaut is building. We learn that expenditures in applied social science research have grown from $235 million in 1965 to $1 billion in 1975; that the number of social scientists has increased by 163 percent from 1960 to 1970; that Congress has accumulated a large professional staff; and that universities are now describing many of their activities as policy related.

Reflection on these facts, however, suggests a modest level of growth for a small institution—hardly the emergence of a juggernaut. A billion dollars represents less than 3 percent of the civilian payroll for the federal government.[1] If we assume that somewhere between 10 and 15 percent of these officials work at policy levels, and if we assume that all this money supports independent policy-related research activity which has as much chance of influencing agency choices as does the work of officials within the agencies, then we can conclude that social science research now constitutes from one-third to one-fifth of the policy-level activity in the federal government. Actually, since social science research products are used quite selectively by agency officials, their real influence probably is much smaller than indicated by this comparison. Furthermore, even if we imagine that *all* the social science research money supports a group of social scientists thinking about policy problems, those social scientists still are significantly outnumbered by salaried government officials and elected representatives.

Similarly, while the number of social scientists grew 163 percent over the decade 1960–1970, the number of personnel and labor specialists grew by 295 percent, and the number of social and recreation workers grew by 230 percent. Moreover, the number of social scientists is now less than 5 percent of the total number of government employees.[2]

Finally, the fact that a few relatively small academic institutions have begun to justify their activities in a period of financial difficulty by claiming that they make a major contribution to social policy hardly indicates either a change in the pattern of universities' activities or an increase in their ability to influence government policy. In short, Banfield's observations fall far short of documenting the emergence of a major new institution.

In fact, Banfield himself presents a great deal of evidence showing that social science has failed to have much impact on the policy process. We hear that "Congress is almost totally impervious to systematic analysis"; that the useful results of a decade of social science

---

[1] U.S. Office of Management and Budget, *Special Analyses: Budget of the U.S. Government—Fiscal Year 1977*, p. 154, table H–3.
[2] U.S. Department of Commerce, *Characteristics of the Population: U.S. Summary*, vol. 1, pt. 1, sec. 2, table 221, 1973.

were "insufficient for a short article, not to speak of a handbook"; and that formal analytic models answered only questions that "nobody was asking." Having assembled these findings, Banfield sums up: "What has been said so far should relieve any reader who might have feared that policy scientists are exercising undue influence. In fact, they have very little influence, certainly very little of a direct kind." It appears, then, that the institution is far from a colossus. Of course, it may be cold comfort to discover that the institution is merely a waste rather than a major threat to the polity; but, still, it *is* comfort—at least when compared to Professor Banfield's apocalyptic view.

Having made social science's irrelevance to actual policy choices part of his case against its potential contribution to the political process, Banfield then has difficulty making us feel seriously threatened by the field's growth. His solution is to warn of disastrous consequences for governmental policy making *if* the institution of social science ever should become influential. In this prospect he sees two distinct threats. One is a significant reduction in the quality of substantive political debates (arising from the difficulty of capturing the world relevant to those debates within social science models). The other is the possibility that social science will create "problems, not solutions." Banfield offers no empirical evidence for these views, but since they are predictions about future trends, this is not unreasonable. What is less reasonable is that he fails to consider the possibility that the influence of social science might develop in a different and more benign direction. Given the uncertainty in the world, surely it is appropriate to consider a variety of potential scenarios.

With respect to the prospect of social science's introducing crude reductionism into policy deliberations, I think there is some possibility that Banfield is right. This is far from certain, however. I can conceive of decision makers remaining aware of the real dimensions of the policy problems they face, even as they learn to be effective interpreters of social science findings and analytic reasoning. We sometimes refer to such people as effective consumers of social science, but it probably would be better to think of them as mediators between the simplified, structured world of social scientists and formal modelers and the messy particular worlds that are the realm of policy decisions. One might call them exceptional clinicians—able to draw on recent findings and theory from a science related to their professional work, but also concerned with each specific case that arises. If enough such people existed, social science could easily enrich rather than impoverish our policy deliberations. Only a philistine could object to the use of carefully collected evidence and closely reasoned analyses of policy options in making decisions—particularly if the raw products of social science research were organized and presented in a form that allowed effective public discussion. Our present problem may be not an excess of social science, but a lack of people who can use it intelligently and effectively in evaluating policy choices.

Exactly what kinds of individuals will be able to accomplish this mediation, and what forms of analysis will be developed to bridge the gap between social science and effective policy choice, remain somewhat unclear. The mediators and forms of analysis that ultimately evolve are not likely to be "scientific" in the narrow sense, but they also will probably look very different from unaided intuition and common sense. My hunch is that both the individuals and the works will bear traces of social science influence, but that the most sophisticated forms of social science will have been abandoned in favor of methods more likely to capture the real subtlety and complexity of the world and to allow—even invite—a broader policy debate. I hesitate to give examples, and I think the two works I have in mind are probably a little too general to be valuable in particular policy situations, but something like *The Unheavenly City* or *Thinking About Crime* might be just what is required. Certainly such works suggest that social science findings can contribute a great deal to effective policy debates, and hence to effective governance.

With respect to the prediction that social science will create problems, not solutions, the argument is somewhat more complex. Note that Banfield believes that the proliferation of problems arises from two different sources: first, social scientists' tendency to discover social problems where they do not exist, and second, their tendency to find fault with old solutions. Together these inclinations ensure a large and frustrating government agenda. My own view, however, is that social scientists produce this result because they are tempted to act not as scientists, but as activists, and because we have unreasonable expectations about how policy decisions could be made.

Consider, first, the prediction that growth in the institution of social science will be accompanied by the discovery of new social problems that require governmental attention. This in itself is not a bad thing. After all, if we learn of a condition that is inconsistent with our communal aspirations, if we can imagine an effective governmental remedy, and if the remedy violates no fundamental conceptions of humanity and erodes no basic institution, then there should be no bar to action. We might praise rather than criticize the person who documented the problem. Only frivolous additions to the government's agenda warrant criticism of the role of social science.

I would also suggest that social science is more likely to debunk claims about emergent social problems than to support them. Science is a profoundly conservative mode of thought: it requires a great deal of observation, evidence, and reasoning to establish the validity of a statement. In fact, if we had insisted on scientific evidence of a health hazard from automobile emissions or of an increase in the number of heroin users, we might never have regulated automobile emissions or declared a war on drugs. Thus, one can contend that a firm commitment to social science would shrink rather than enlarge the government's agenda.

It is sometimes argued that the social scientists who "find" social problems are not really acting as scientists: they are advocates, or propagandists. But the fact that this role is common today tells us more about the weakness of professional norms governing social scientists, and the gullibility (whether ingenuous or not) of public officials, than about the inherent tendencies of social science. The position of social scientists who act as propagandists is a weak one; if they could be bound to higher professional standards, and if public officials were independently capable of evaluating their arguments, their tendency to "find" frivolous problems could be stopped.

According to Banfield, the second way social science contributes problems rather than solutions is by finding fault with old solutions and adding complexity to current conceptions of problems. Reflection reveals that this is the flip side of the coin of the conservatism of science. In evaluating past policies or designing new initiatives, social science does play a spoiler's role. Because conservative rules of evidence make it hard to conclude that a policy's desired effect actually has occurred, evaluations of governmental programs nearly always fail to show any effect. This scientific skepticism may indeed create frustration and—sometimes, at least—a sense of governmental incompetence. But it is also a powerful means of pruning the reach of government, disciplining its ambitions, and redirecting its efforts toward more successful approaches. We have seen social science play this role in several recent issues: rehabilitation in the criminal justice system, various kinds of regulation, and many of the initiatives of the Great Society. Learning that previous goals were too ambitious or that previous means were poorly designed is cause for frustration and despair only if we thought at the beginning that we were acting with precision on the basis of perfect information. If we understand that social science cannot guarantee an effective policy design, though it can determine how a given approach has performed, we will not be disappointed or frustrated so frequently, and we certainly will not blame social science for our frustrations.

Thus, social science need not be an engine for enlarging the scope or compounding the frustrations of governmental action. As a profoundly conservative force, it can debunk claims that problems exist, and it can show the inadequacy of current governmental efforts. If we take science seriously when it decides that problems exist, and if we use it to help us learn something about the impact of past and present policies, it can become a force for shrinking the government's agenda and redirecting its efforts rather than for expanding the governmental quagmire.

My final point in rebuttal to Banfield's claim that social science is a dangerous emergent estate is somewhat different. Even if Banfield's predictions about the development of social science should prove accurate, it is not clear that the problems he anticipates would be results of the internal dynamics of social science. My suspicion is that the growth of social science is not a cause but a consequence of much more fundamental problems of governance.

One such problem is simply that citizens expect much more from their government now than ever before. They seek representation and expression not only on the bases of their occupational roles, but also as individuals who are concerned about the shape of their lives outside their jobs. They want good health, safety, and recreation, as well as economic and civil security. And they want these things not only for themselves, but for larger and larger groups in the society. Government has responded with an array of new programs—which policy makers desperately need help in designing and running. It is as a source of this help that social scientists have become important, an easily expanded work force that can assist government in responding to citizen demands. They may look as though they are forcing the development of the government's programs, but nothing would change if we temporarily shattered the institution. The reason for the expansion is not social science, but a shift in people's expectations.

A second problem is related to the first, but it is less fundamental. Public officials and representatives have shown a discouraging tendency to rely on social science in making choices.[3] When faced with difficult choices, they seem to prefer to hide behind apparently scientific arguments that support their position—to substitute technique and credentials for judgment and character. This is unfortunate because each time they do so, they sustain a false idea of what social science can be expected to accomplish. The politician's need for scientific justification could account for the growth of social science rather than any internal dynamic within social science itself.

In sum, then, it has not been shown convincingly that science is very influential, nor that such influence as it has is necessarily

---

[3] I am indebted to Gary Orren for emphasizing this point.

harmful, nor that its growth can be attributed to its own internal dynamics. The institution has some potential for harm and some for good. It is not yet fixed on one track or the other. The problem is to harness it on behalf of effective governance.

### Statesmanship and Programs in Public Policy

Two persistent themes have run throughout this essay. One is that much of the work of government is confronting complex substantive choices, a situation that is likely to continue for the indefinite future. This circumstance probably arises not from the growth of social science but from other, more fundamental causes. A second theme is that social science is neither a substitute for nor a major threat to public officials' ability to think intelligently and responsibly about the decisions they face. To the extent that formal applications of social science come to dominate policy debates, there is some risk that debate will be substantively and procedurally impoverished. But it is not clear that any sensible policy maker would allow this to happen. Nor is it clear that the institution of social science is inclined or able to force itself on the policy process. On the other hand, if we ignore the findings of social scientists, or fail to appreciate social science's capacity for using rigorous logic and carefully assembled empirical information in reasoning about policy problems, we risk thinking about these problems less effectively than we might.

Under these circumstances, the possibilities for statesmanlike decisions might be enhanced by the development of structures and processes that mediate between the institution of social science and the policy process. I do not want to exaggerate the importance of establishing such links; the relationship between social science and the policy process is only one of many factors that affect the prospects for statesmanship. But in a world of particular substantive choices and a growing social science establishment, this relationship is becoming *relatively* more important. As a result, managing this relationship is gradually becoming a priority matter.

The establishment of a link between social science and policy deliberations is likely to depend on two related developments. One is the emergence of a group of people whose work is deliberating practical policies, but who also have a sophisticated understanding of the methods of social science. This combined capacity is important for at least three reasons. First, their facility with social science methods can enlarge these people's ability to reason about policy problems. Second, their understanding of the methods can enable them to use the raw products of social science with ease and discrimination. Third, their commitment to the largely political and procedural world of particular policy choices can keep them from sacrificing important institutional relationships and values for limited substantive objectives. Such individuals thus can bind the worlds of social science and policy choice together without sacrificing the ethos of either.

A second crucial development is the creation of forms of reasoning that draw on the sophisticated analytic and empirical methods of social science, but that are at the same time comprehensible to those who have a stake in policy choices. The raw products of social science research so admired by professionals for their methodological competence must somehow be transformed into sensible policy arguments allowing broad political discussion. Of course, the development of these forms of analysis will be facilitated by the emergence of people with both practical and social science skills. It is likely that this group will have to take responsibility for creating the forms and policing the practice as well. They must become self-conscious about their role and communicate their standards to others. In short, a modest professional group may have to emerge to mediate between the world of politics and the world of social science.

Encouraging these developments is the purpose of most public policy programs with which I am acquainted. They are designed to facilitate the emergence of a group of people who feel ultimately responsible to the political process, but who are sophisticated about social science. They are also concerned with creating forms of analysis that are informed by social science methods and findings *and* that present a picture of the world familiar to those with both knowledge of and a stake in that world. Thus, to the extent that public policy programs succeed in their ambitions, we can expect the relationship between social science and the policy process to be managed more effectively in the future. And, to the extent that more effective management of this relationship enhances the prospects for statesmanlike decisions in a world of particular policy choices, public policy programs will contribute to rather than lessen the prospects for statesmanship.

# 3

# Policy Analysis: Boon or Curse for Politicians?

*Laurence H. Silberman*

That the federal bureaucracy has become relatively impervious to political control is, I think, undeniable. I would contend, however, that this circumstance has little to do with politicians' growing dependence on policy analysis. The problem is rather that politicians and political appointees rarely bring to office coherent notions of governance. Bureaucrats, naturally, defend their "turf" tenaciously and seek expansion of their programs virtually without regard to past effectiveness. And government bureaucrats, like any other bureaucrats (or, indeed, any other people), are quick to seize on new program possibilities that promise general advancement—again, virtually without regard to likely results. Unless we try massive lobotomies, we are unlikely to change behavior so rooted in human nature. We are, however, entitled to rely on political authority—the president and his direct appointees, as well as Congress—to channel bureaucratic energies toward reasonably useful goals. But if our political authorities cannot muster a clear and interrelated vision of these goals, control of the bureaucracy is an illusion.

Throughout the twentieth century, our political scientists and journalists have exalted political pragmatism—practical problem solving—as opposed to ideology. The "isms"—Marxism, fascism, Spencerian capitalism—all of which are characterized by theoretical explanations encompassing all human behavior, have so frightened our politicians and political observers that they shy away from any theoretical concepts of government. Condemnation of ideology leads to distrust of broad coherent notions of what government should and should not try to accomplish. Instead, the "neutral" problem solvers are much in demand. Jimmy Carter, the engineer president, is an archetype of that breed. Ad hoc problem solving, however, is not governance—at least, not effective governance. Unless a president brings into office a coherent notion of what he wishes to accomplish as well as a body of presidential appointees who largely share that notion, the bureaucracy—indeed, the entire government—will drift aimlessly—or, perhaps more accurately, grow aimlessly.

Washington wags are fond of saying that it takes only a few months for a presidential appointee to be captured by the bureaucracy he or she (hereafter he) is charged with supervising. Regretfully, in my experience, the cliché has more than a little truth in it. That co-optation is inevitable if an appointee has no independent, preappointment view of desirable agency goals, closely connected with overall administration policy. Lacking such a view, he lacks any conceptual framework with which to compare agency practice. Issues brought to the appointee by civil servants will rarely call into question the fundamental aims of the agency; typically, they will instead be marginal or incremental questions which assume the propriety and wisdom of all that has gone before. After making only a few decisions in response to such questions and issues, the appointee is hopelessly ensnared in a psychological trap: he has implicitly accepted—indeed, internalized—agency history and become a defender of the faith.

Since defending the bureaucracy is infinitely less taxing to the politician than challenging it—if he defends it, he is constantly buoyed by assurances from his subordinates and colleagues that he is a wonderful administrator—doing so gives him extra energy with which to make his mark in Washington. He turns inevitably to new policy initiatives that will expand his agency's mission and thereby his own bureaucratic sway. New initiatives normally are encased in legislative proposals, whether or not the same steps could be taken administratively, because in Washington passing legislation is an end rather than a means to an end. That is, virtually all political credit accrues at the time legislation is passed establishing a new program ("great victory over forces of darkness," etc.). Political observers, particularly journalists, find the subsequent question of how well a program is administered too boring for close attention.

Does the advent of policy analysis—this new branch of social "science"—worsen the situation, as Professor Banfield so elegantly argues? Central to his gloomy view is his prediction that policy analysts eventually will dominate both executive and legislative branch bureaucracies and will overawe and befuddle politicians with their techniques. My own view is that the issue of control turns on the quality of the politicians or political appointees. Since most political appointees already have been captured by their constituent bureaucracies, it is hard to see how policy analysis can weaken their effectiveness. On the other hand, if a politician enters into his duties with a sufficiently well-formed notion of what he wants to accomplish, policy analysis can be very helpful.

Policy analysis, as I understand it, is a form of applied economics—a set of methods for attempting to measure the costs and benefits of various policy choices, or evaluate the efficacy of existing government programs, in economic or quantitative terms. Policy analysts are prone to excessive use of overly sophisticated mathematical techniques of dubious utility, no doubt; but at bottom, policy analysis is merely a device for evaluating government actions (actual or proposed) that cannot be measured by marketplace tests.

For several reasons, government bureaucracies do not like to be measured. First, many programs pursue conflicting legislative goals, even mutually inconsistent ones, which evaluation may force those in charge to reconcile. Second, measurement or evaluation is inherently threatening to anyone, because it introduces the risk that changes will be made on the basis of the results. Third, government bureaucrats tend to believe that their program efforts are useful whether or not they have evidence of any impact on supposed beneficiaries, a conviction measurement may shatter.

A good policy analyst brought into government will instinctively begin to measure existing programs—indeed, most are hired for that very purpose.[1] This means that analysts generally assume an adversary posture in relation to the program bureaucracies, a posture that grows naturally out of their training as well as function. This adversary relationship between those who administer programs and those who measure them is of enormous importance to the political appointee who wishes to control a government bureaucracy. Without it, even the most determined politician-manager has little chance to lay bare the fundamental questions underlying a program. Only through a systematic evaluation can a political appointee bring out and grasp the crucial substructure beneath the apparent problems he

---

[1] In 1971, shortly after I became undersecretary of labor, I asked senior officials in the Manpower Administration which of their programs seemed most successful at preparing the chronically unemployed for the labor market. Despite almost a decade of experience and billions of spent dollars, they had no answer—indeed, they found the question quite threatening. After that, I sought to build a group of tough-minded evaluators to answer that kind of question. Macroeconomists, brought into government temporarily from academia, were generally the best at it (which has led me to believe that macroeconomists are wonderful for all sorts of government work—except macroeconomic planning). Several years later, as deputy attorney general, I started similar structures at the Justice Department, for like reasons.

faces. He may well believe on entering office that a government program is misconceived, but analysis is important to add conviction and legitimacy to his views.

The adversary relationship between the policy analysts and program bureaucrats, which grows out of the former's evaluation function, carries over to policy formulation. Here too it is of significant help to the political appointee, because it tends to produce *real* policy choices, without which management (control) is very difficult. Even the best politician-manager, if forced to struggle continually against a virtually monolithic bureaucracy, eventually will begin to adopt traditional solutions to new problems. He will be too worn down psychologically to advance his own ideas. A creative tension between policy analysts and line bureaucrats liberates the appointee, not only to choose between different approaches but to fashion his own. It is not so much, then, that policy analysts present policy alternatives superior to those offered by the traditional bureaucracy; it is rather that the process of policy analysis tends to broaden choices—and often, I might add, to include a prudent "do nothing" option.

But does their very usefulness give policy analysts undue influence over politicians? Will the policy analysts' options carry disproportionate legitimacy because they are "scientific"? Not in my experience. Indeed, I can recall no instance of a politician's accepting a product of policy analysis that deviated sharply from politically acceptable solutions. In that respect the program bureaucracy has an enormous advantage; it can always muster political force behind its proposals by rallying a constituency with which it enjoys a symbiotic relationship. The truth is that any solution (or problem) proposed by policy analysts that runs contrary to prevailing political winds has only a very slim chance of acceptance.

The crux of Professor Banfield's concern seems to be the likelihood that all bureaucrats eventually will be trained in policy analysis and that this development, over time, will increasingly frustrate political control. Who will challenge the bureaucracy when it is armed with this formidable new weapon? The answer, in part, is policy analysis itself. So long as separate groups are maintained to perform evaluation functions, the adversary relationship I have described will continue to operate. That line bureaucrats may speak the same language as policy analysts will not insulate them from inquiry and measurement.

Moreover, I am more sanguine than Professor Banfield that politicians can, by learning the strengths and weaknesses of policy analysis, exercise appropriate control over its use. First, the politician must control the questions put to policy analysts—not to such an extreme that he is unwilling to consider the analysts' views as to what questions *can* be answered, but to the extent that he and not the analysts (or anyone else) sets the policy agenda. The person who asks the operative questions directs policy analysis. For that direction to be an appropriate one, however, the questions must be relevant to the overall policy of the political authorities. Again I emphasize that if the politician is not guided by a coherent policy aim, control of any part of the bureaucracy, including the policy analysts, is out of the question.

Second, the politician must be prepared to seize the product of policy analysis when *he* needs it, not when the policy analyst believes it sufficiently complete to withstand academic criticism. Policy analysts are often reluctant to provide preliminary data from sensitive evaluations for fear that politicians will "run" with the data and use them in making administrative, legislative, or budget decisions before the analysts are comfortable with their conclusions. The policy analyst typically does not understand that resolution of policy questions cannot always wait for a polished product. In the absence of preliminary evaluation data, the politician's decision will be based on even less reliable anecdotal impressions. In other words, the best is often the mortal enemy of the good.

Third, the timing and mode of publication of the product of policy analysis cannot be left for the policy analysts to determine unilaterally. This is not to say that a politician can successfully suppress government-spawned policy studies that contradict his preconceived or politically directed "line"; indeed, should he try to do so, the attempt is almost certain to be frustrated by leaks. Still, if the politician permits the policy analyst to control publication, he abdicates his right and duty to attempt to persuade the public of his policy views.

Finally, the politician must always keep in mind that policy analysis is not magic. In the event that his honest conviction is at odds with what policy analysis tells him, he does better to stick with his own judgment. That assumes, of course, that his is an honest view. Policy analysts are wont to say that a politician's appreciation of the limits of policy analysis follows quickly on his recognition that a given product deviates from the dominant political consensus. There is much truth to that complaint; but in a democracy, that is as it should be.

I do not mean to suggest that the politician should treat policy analysis or policy analysts cynically, simply as arrows to be fired at his own preselected targets. Policy analysis produces facts—or probable facts, or possible facts; the politician who is unwilling to modify

41

his view in the face of facts that on balance seem reliable is merely an ideologue—surely not a candidate for statesman. No; I believe policy analysts should be afforded respect as professionals whose contribution can be important. That is not inconsistent with insisting on political control of them as of other bureaucrats.

In sum, although I very much fear the inexorable, aimless growth of government, I do not fear the increasing popularity of policy analysis, because I do not see it as a contributing cause of that aimless bureaucratic growth. On the contrary, I am convinced that politicians with a central purpose—those who seek office not to preside but to govern—can use policy analysis as an important aid in pursuit of their purpose.

It has been contended that supporters of policy analysis cannot point to any successes. I would argue that, particularly in the field of evaluation, policy analysis has had a significant impact. A number of federal programs, including virtually the whole range of Great Society initiatives, has been significantly discredited by evaluation. To be sure, many of these programs remain in spite of the negative evaluations; some have even expanded. But others have been cut or redirected (particularly those operated by the Office of Economic Opportunity, the Department of Housing and Urban Development, the Manpower Administration, and the Law Enforcement Assistance Administration). That we have not been more successful in eliminating the worst programs is hardly the fault of policy analysis. The fault lies with the American people, who cling tenaciously to the illusion that if government spends enough money trying to solve a problem—whether crime, unemployment, or bad housing—that spending will inevitably have a beneficial impact. Still, the failure of the Great Society programs, which was demonstrated by evaluation, has had its political effect; the so-called neoconservative movement seems to spring largely from a widespread, perhaps pervasive realization of government's inherent limitations, a realization to which policy analysis has contributed. The result, at minimum, is that new government initiatives must cross a higher political threshold than before.

When initiatives do go forward now, they are more likely to be constructed in such a way that they can be evaluated fairly readily once underway. Line bureaucrats and politicians thus are implicitly induced to state clearly the goals of any new program, because otherwise it is impossible to measure that program's success or failure. The intellectual discipline involved in that process works against half-baked government adventurism. Of course, the policy analyst does thereby gain more influence over program design—he or she often argues for smaller tentative steps that can be evaluated before large resources are committed. In my judgment, this kind of prudence should be welcomed.

Policy analysis (or research), as Professor Banfield argues, does seem to add to the complexity of problems. But I find that comforting, rather than troubling, since it tends to give politicians some pause before they launch new initiatives based, as in the 1960s, on simplistic notions of the efficacy of government intervention. The more we realize that everything in human behavior relates to everything else, the less we may be impelled to try, through government instrumentalities, to make drastic alterations in certain aspects of that behavior.

George Will recently observed that much of modern government springs from a persistent human drive to repeal economic laws derived from human nature and the nature of society. Policy analysis, properly used, acts in a limited way to counter that drive. Admittedly, it is more effective at revealing past government errors than at devising new government programs. The reason is obvious: government efforts to repeal economic laws invariably fail.

# 4

# Policy Analysis and Public Choice

*Gustave H. Shubert*

The theme of this volume is that there is a difference, fundamental but imprecisely defined, between "statesman" and "bureaucrat," and a perceived need to increase both the number and the influence of the former to reverse the trend toward dominance of the latter in making public choices. To oversimplify, I define the statesman as a wise man, one who rises selflessly above the level of bureaucratic infighting—and, in some sense, politics itself—to make policy decisions and recommendations on the basis of principle and knowledge, regardless of the consequences to himself or to the coalition of forces that has made him a decision maker. The bureaucrat, on the other hand, prototypically defined as a rather narrow, sometimes base fellow, is viewed as spending most of his time warding off attacks on his predetermined policy positions (that is, more security, more budget, more power, etc.), avoiding difficult choices, and, when forced to make a tough decision affecting the public welfare, doing so on the basis of his judgment about the consequences of the decisions for his own job, his own sphere of influence, and the narrowly defined goals and interests of his organizational base—in that order.

## The Goals of Policy Analysis

Having worked with one or two such "statesmen," and having met more than one such "bureaucrat," I suspect that the number of individuals falling into these categories is (and ought to be) much smaller than might be suspected. In any case, whatever the validity of this extreme caricature (an issue addressed more directly by other authors in this volume), and quite apart from my own beliefs about the proper limitations on the power and prerogatives of government, whether by statesman or bureaucrat, it is my thesis that policy analysis can be and has been useful in helping bureaucrats and statesmen alike in making better decisions. Indeed, policy analysis, far from increasing the ability of the bureaucrat to dominate the policy process, can help both statesmen and bureaucrats to work together "in the public interest." Through properly and publicly conducted policy analysis, decisions can be made and issues posed in such a way that the probable consequences of choices are more fully taken into account, both by officials and by the public.

Informing decisions is, in fact, the central purpose of policy analysis. A young science, policy analysis seeks to combine the most advanced skills of the traditional disciplines and to focus them on policy problems. The goal is not to provide "solutions" (although the search for "dominance" will always remain part of the policy analyst's dream). Rather, the goal is to ensure that the problem itself is understood (by asking the right questions) and defined (by specifying its parameters); that relevant and reliable information is available to be used in addressing the problem (by using secondary sources as well as generating primary data, if necessary); that a spectrum of alternative solutions is included in the analysis; that the effects of each alternative and their distribution, including benefits and costs, are projected and the degree of uncertainty surrounding each projection is specified; and that both the assumptions of the analysis and the criteria of evaluation are unambiguously stated. Ideally, the results of the analysis will be communicated in such a way that the policy makers, both statesmen and bureaucrats, can assign their own values and use their own judgment in weighting outcomes along such disparate and often orthogonal measures as, for example, environmental impact versus relative abundance of energy, or total costs versus distribution of costs.

The successful conduct of high-quality policy analysis requires above all that people with solid training in appropriate disciplines do the work; that they be able to work together across disciplinary lines; and that they communicate effectively among themselves and with their peers. Their work should be carefully and intensively reviewed by their colleagues before it is communicated to the policy maker to ensure not only that it meets the quality standards specified above but also that it meets the principal criterion of scientific analysis— "re-creatability."

Re-creatability may be, in fact, the principal difference between applied common sense and policy analysis. It requires not only that the analysts have a model of the world, but also that that model be specified in such a way that the connections between assumption and conclusion, between knowledge and conclusion, and between theory and conclusion are all made specific, enabling the decision makers to understand the analysis and to re-create it on the basis of their own assumptions, knowledge, and values—a crucial test of what might often be deemed the face validity of analysis, quantitative or not.

## The Uses of Policy Analysis

Earlier I asserted that policy analysis has had and will continue to have a beneficial influence on major policy decisions. I believe this to be true at all levels of government—federal, state, and local. If I support this contention largely with examples from Rand's experience it is not because Rand is unique, or preeminent, or has solved the problem of connecting systematic analysis with policy decisions and these decisions with improvements in the quality of life; I do so because I am most familiar with the conduct and impact of Rand work.

**New York City Housing.** Let me turn first to an example of an analysis of a public policy problem—housing—that spans all three levels of government and has affected the ways in which statesmen, bureaucrats, and the general public think about the problem as well as government decisions themselves. The initial work was conducted from 1968 to 1971 by the New York City-Rand Institute and focused on the housing problems of the city per se. New York City conducts and regulates housing programs on a scale exceeded only by the federal government. At the time of our study, the city's public housing agency had half a million tenants; another 85,000 rental units had been built and were regulated under state- or city-financed middle-income housing programs. About 70 percent of all the city's rental units and nearly half of all housing units had been under rent control since 1943, a program administered by the city since 1962.

The Rand analysis[1] of the city's housing problems helped change policy makers' perceptions in a number of fundamental ways. It set the scene by providing *for the first time* a comprehensive presentation of all housing programs—federal, state, and local—affecting the city's housing stock, pointing out not only the enormousness of total resources devoted to the city's housing "problem," but also the diver-

---

[1] I. S. Lowry, ed., *Rental Housing in New York City*, Vol. 1, Confronting the Crisis. Rand Memorandum RM-6190-NYC (Santa Monica, Calif.: The Rand Corporation, February 1970). A bibliography of the reports and papers from this project is in the *Final Report, 1969–1976, The New York City-Rand Institute* (Santa Monica, Calif.: The Rand Corporation, 1977), pp. 26–27, 60–61.

sity of application of those resources and the unexpectedly powerful leverage the city's own resources could have on those from state and federal sources.

The analysis proceeded to redefine the "problem." Up to that point, the city's housing problems had ordinarily been formulated in terms of how to build enough new housing from the ground up to meet the demand for housing services. After preliminary studies, however, the analysts realized that New York City was annually losing more housing units through deterioration and abandonment (38,000 units a year between 1965 and 1967) than it could possibly build. The impact of this situation on citizens and on the city treasury was significant in terms of emergency services, housing relocation costs, and tax losses, as well as in secondary effects in such areas as fire, sanitation, and crime. Working with the staff of the city's Housing and Development Administration, the Institute was able to cause a major shift in priorities, from concentration on new construction as the assumed solution to the housing crisis to the problem of preservation of the existing housing stock.

The most controversial and important of our recommendations was reform of a sacred cow, the city's antiquated system of rent controls, which essentially reflected 1943 costs. Continuing imposition of these controls meant that rental revenues were insufficient to support adequate maintenance over the long term, leading to widespread deterioration and abandonment. Further, the controls were not designed to benefit low-income tenants, but rather made their effects felt in an arbitrary way across the income spectrum.

The Institute recommended that rent controls be restructured, with rent ceilings being gradually raised to levels that would permit adequate maintenance while yielding a fair return on the owner's investment. A formula for these increases was also devised, reflecting the specific characteristics of each building and apartment. In addition, rent assistance for residents unable to afford the full cost of adequate housing was proposed, again with attention to programmatic detail. Finally, an organized effort to locate and salvage properties in serious difficulty because of poor management or inadequate revenue was suggested as an alternative to punitive regulation or to tax foreclosure and city ownership by default.

The Institute's housing strategy report was received with extreme caution by the city, which used its release as a trial balloon (in the basket of which, by the way, the Rand Institute was the only passenger). Rent control reforms were eventually passed by the City Council essentially as proposed by the Institute. The mayor, his statesmanship shaped and supported by a compelling quantitative analysis, confronted the state and secured an agreement to implement those reforms. Although their implementation was subsequently plagued both by administrative difficulties and by counterreforms instituted by the state legislature, the laws were changed so as to increase the incentives of landlords to operate and to maintain decent, safe, and sanitary housing instead of continuing to disinvest through undermaintenance, deterioration, and outright abandonment.

**The Housing Assistance Supply Experiment.** Moreover, the Institute's proposal for rent assistance to low-income families attracted attention at the federal level, and as a result Rand designed and is now conducting an experiment for the U.S. Department of Housing and Urban Development (HUD).[2] The experiment is designed to help HUD and the Congress decide whether a national program of direct cash assistance to low-income households is a feasible and desirable way to help them secure decent housing in a suitable living environment; and, if so, to help determine the best terms and conditions for such assistance and the most efficient and appropriate methods for administering a nationwide program. The principal hypothesis being tested is that *direct* cash assistance to families and individuals—thus placing them on the demand side of the housing market—is more effective and efficient than the more traditional subsidies to landlords or to public housing agencies.

The Housing Assistance Supply Experiment is a full-scale, ten-year allowance program in two metropolitan areas chosen for strong contrasts in their housing markets, Brown County, Wisconsin (whose central city is Green Bay) and St. Joseph County, Indiana (whose central city is South Bend). The most important conclusion reached thus far is that neither market was noticeably disrupted by the enrollment of several thousand low-income families during the first year of program operations. No evidence has been found that the program caused inflation in rents or home prices; generated real estate speculation, home repair fraud, or high neighborhood turnover; or aroused widespread hostility toward participants or toward the program itself. These findings contradict the position of many "statesmen" who have argued that construction of subsidized housing is the only way to meet national housing goals.

The other side of the coin is that the program so far has not dramatically affected housing expenditures; the amount of housing construction and home repair; neighborhood quality; the policies of

---

[2] *Fourth Annual Report of the Housing Assistance Supply Experiment,* Rand Report R-2302-HUD (Santa Monica, Calif.: The Rand Corporation, May 1978).

landlords, mortgage lenders, or realtors; the degree of residential segregation; or tenure arrangements.

The participants themselves, however, have benefited in two ways. First, their financial burdens have been eased by allowance payments. When they enrolled, nearly all were spending more than a fourth of their income for housing; many spent as much as 40 or 50 percent. Now, only the poorest participants spend much more than a fourth of nonallowance income for housing. Second, about a third are occupying better housing, sometimes because they have moved, but more often because they have repaired their homes to meet program standards. A few renters have bought homes with the aid of the allowance.

In short, this program has so far been modestly successful in meeting its main objective: enabling participants to afford decent, safe, and sanitary housing without unreasonably scrimping on other forms of consumption. As far as we can tell now, program costs are lower than those of traditional government housing programs. Community benefits—such as visible neighborhood improvements or the residential integration of minorities—remain more elusive. The program may or may not be able to achieve these effects. Any such benefits will have to come slowly, over the next several years.

## The Conduct of Policy Analysis

The Housing Assistance Supply Experiment suggests several insights into the general conduct of policy analysis. First, when a government agency seeks analytical help, the agency often specifies in great detail what it believes the problem to be for which the policy analyst is to find an answer. But often this definition of the problem masks the real problem. Discovering the real problem is one of the policy analyst's most important challenges. Since there is no gain in getting a precise answer to the wrong question, the analyst must have intellectual elbow room, as well as a commitment to the real world. The government agency does itself a disservice when it specifies too narrowly the question to be studied. Close interaction between analyst and agency from the very beginning can bring about one of the most important results of policy analysis: persuading the government official (most often the bureaucrat?) to ask the right question, as well as suggesting to the government official (most often the statesman?) that he may not already have the "right" answer.

Second, problems in the real world do not come classified neatly—this one for the economist, that one for the engineer, and so on. Rather, it is necessary that analysts from many disciplines learn

49

to work together effectively. In the Housing Assistance Supply Experiment economists, statisticians, sociologists, computer analysts, operations researchers, and anthropologists are working together. Each must understand the other disciplines, must come to understand the conceptual models of the others, must learn how to communicate across disciplinary lines, and must help integrate the work of all so that it may be understood and assessed by government officials, and so that its conclusions may be implemented in the midst of full public awareness.

Third, social experiments such as the Housing Assistance Supply Experiment (and the Income Maintenance Experiments and the Health Insurance Experiment) require time—time to design, time to conduct, time to analyze—and government officials themselves must have at least as much patience as the experimenters have a sense of urgency. Early or intermediate results can be misleading. Some qualified balance must be reached between those who demand instant answers to long and continuing social problems and those who would stop the world until their analyses have been perfected.

Fourth, there are problems in estimating the period during which it is reasonable to expect some direct effect of policy analysis, quite aside from its indirect effect. In cases where, for example, the policy maker violently and publicly rejects not only the analysis and its conclusions but also the analysts themselves (as happened in Rand's work on several aspects of urban police performance[3]) it would seem unreasonable to expect any impact at all, ever. Yet in this case, major changes in resource allocation, in measuring police performance, in force deployment, and in recruiting practices can be traced to the work of Rand's disfranchised and disenchanted policy analysts, although the changes were for the most part billed by the police department as originating from within.

In other cases, immediate direct effects might reasonably be expected but may never occur. The timing may be right, the problem important, the analysis compelling, and yet other considerations may dominate, often quite properly. Consider, for example, Rand's analysis of how best to organize and administer a combined health services agency for the state of California. Rand was asked at the time the department was being formed what objectives would be appropriate for the agency, how it ought to allocate its resources among those objectives and with what priorities, what sorts of personnel and organization made sense, and other key questions. This analysis, in spite of all the conditions in its favor, has had little if any effect

---

[3] *Final Report, 1969–1976*, pp. 13–17, 62–63.

beyond reminding the department that at one point it did want and need to assess itself and its effectiveness. A new "statesman," who believed he had all the answers, arrived on the scene and rejected Rand's analysis. Subsequently the department was broken up.

Most cases, however, fall between these extremes. But in any event, the timing of direct impact, and consequently the time at which measurement of the "value" of policy analysis will be accurate, is uncertain.

**New York City Welfare.** Welfare, like the rest of New York City's problems, has been as unwieldy as it has been elusive of solution. It is unwieldy because of its magnitude: in 1973, as the New York City-Rand Institute began a critical phase of its analysis of this problem, 17 percent of the city's population, or 1.25 million persons, were receiving welfare. By January 1974, the city had 74 percent of the state's and 8 percent of the nation's welfare population. The city's welfare problems had been growing rapidly. In ten years (January 1963 to January 1973) the city's welfare caseload more than tripled—from 360,000 to 1,240,000 persons. The city distributed about $17 million in public assistance in January 1963 and about $107 million in January 1973.

Many guesses were made about the poor in New York City—who they were, how they lived, and what steps would best help them. These guesses led to the conviction that employment and job referral programs would be the most effective solution to the problem, but there were surprisingly few hard statistical analyses on which to base sound policies. Supporters of the federal administration's proposed Family Assistance Plan were defeated by proponents of a "get tough" philosophy, again formulated largely on guesses.

At that time the city did not know the distribution of cases by size and composition of family or by the age and sex of welfare recipients. It did not know the average grant received, the number receiving food stamps, the size of shelter allowances, or the sources of nonwelfare income for recipients. It was widely believed that most welfare recipients stay on the rolls so long as to become wholly dependent, but the city had no information on the experience of individuals over time. No one knew how many people were eligible for but not receiving welfare, or who might turn to welfare if the economy worsened.

There were no reliable statistics on how many of those on welfare were employable. Job training and employment programs operated without reliable statistics to show whether they had moved more people from welfare into jobs than would have been the case without the programs. Nor was much known about who received the benefits of the shelter allowance program, the Medicaid program, or the social services program, or about how much recipients got, or whether alternative lower-cost options could be devised. Were recipients of equal need receiving similar benefits, and was the money spent to help the poor actually achieving the stated objectives of each program?

To answer some of these questions, the city asked the New York City-Rand Institute to help in designing and implementing policy studies on welfare clients, their characteristics and patterns of dependence, and the effectiveness of various programs in meeting their needs.

One of the reasons that the city asked Rand for help is that most of the decisions affecting welfare policy are imposed by Washington or Albany without any evaluation by the city of the consequences of these decisions. A set of procedures for estimating the economic impact on the city of welfare policy changes, while they are still at the proposal stage, was needed to aid city administrators in assessing current and future proposals for welfare reform.

As a result of Rand's work,[4] we now know far more about the welfare problem and we know some more about solutions. Some changes have already been made, and others still may come about. One example is in the area of employment. More than 25 percent of the adults on welfare were also full-time members of the work force. The majority of able-bodied persons on welfare wanted to work and did in fact work intermittently, going on welfare only as a last resort or to supplement earnings. That is, there was no substantial number of employable welfare recipients who did not participate in the labor force.

The Institute's studies of job training and employment programs showed massive ineffectiveness. The "statesmen" had voted to require all employable welfare recipients to report to the state employment service to pick up their checks, on the assumption that a little cajoling would increase the number who found their way back to work. One statesman coined the phrase "from the welfare rolls to payrolls." Welfare recipients jammed employment offices, but less than 30 percent were ever referred to a job, and less than 8 percent found jobs—jobs that most would have taken anyway. The Institute's research showed a significant existing movement in and out of employment by welfare recipients, so the mandatory job referral pro-

---

[4] D. W. Lyon, *Welfare Policy Research for New York City: The Record of a Five-Year Project,* Rand Report R-2119-RC (Santa Monica, Calif.: The Rand Corporation, December 1976).

gram had only a slim chance of speeding up the process. The cost of running the job referral program grew, employment offices began to reduce their services to regular clients, and the overall ineffectiveness of the program became apparent. Within three years bureaucrats convinced statesmen of the wrong-headedness of the legislation, and the decision was made to send once again checks directly to employable welfare recipients and provide them job referrals on a first-come, first-served basis. The whole episode could have been avoided if statesmen had seriously considered the facts that bureaucrats and policy analysts provided them.

The Institute also found that the city's shelter allowance policy was both inequitable and expensive. Families with the same need for housing were found to be receiving vastly different allowances for shelter. This research resulted in a major, city-sponsored proposal to the state calling for a flat-grant scheme of rent allowances. In 1975 the state of New York reinstituted a policy of maximum ceilings for each case size along lines suggested by our analysis.

**Computer Simulation.** Another example of intermediate-term impact also illustrates a special kind of methodological transfer—a mathematical model developed in work on national security applied in quite a different field. I have chosen the example because, unlike our earlier examples, it has a strong engineering component, and often the engineer must work closely with the biologist, the economist, and others.

A dozen or so years ago a Rand engineer studied the problems of putting ballistic missiles on ocean platforms, on the surface or underwater. He developed a method of calculating numerically the complicated motions and forces involved when waves hit the platforms. The computer-based model was eventually extended to create mathematical models of water movement in estuaries, where rivers and tides meet in shallow coastal waters. Because a large part of the U.S. population lives close to the major estuaries along the coasts, the dual concerns of water quality and safety from flooding are major issues.

Civil engineers are accustomed to building actual physical models of a harbor area, say, to simulate flow conditions. Such a model can represent the rise and fall of the tides and the effect of wave action, but it cannot take into account other important factors that can be handled by the computer-based numerical model. That is, one is also concerned with water quality, health standards, conservation, airport expansion, dredging, and landfills. Water pollution control needs systematic analyses: what are the effects of the location of sewer

53

outfalls, the effects of the degree of sewage treatment, and so forth. Analysis must include the effects of biochemical processes, bacteria deposition by sedimentation, aeration at the surface, and the effects of heat, together with the local geography, bottom contours, tidal flow, and other factors. The mathematical model can produce predicted impacts quickly and at low cost, and the government can act on them with confidence.

In the late 1960s, for example, the U.S. Army Corps of Engineers proposed to build a hurricane barrier across the Rockaway Inlet to protect the low-lying areas of Jamaica Bay during severe storms. New York City became concerned about the possible effects of the barrier on the bay, a 9,000-acre wetland, in part a wildlife refuge, and an area whose recreational potential has scarcely been realized. In addition, the city wanted to be able to estimate the effects of dredging or landfills within the bay and the effects of planned sewer overflow treatment facilities.

The computer simulation techniques developed at Rand were applied to Jamaica Bay.[5] The main criteria used for assessing changes in water quality were the net circulation in the bay, distribution of coliform bacteria, and the distribution of chlorides and dissolved oxygen. The simulation model showed that the hurricane barrier would create no significant change in water quality; consequently, construction of the barrier is still under consideration. New York City also then had a validated tool with which to estimate the effects of other proposed changes in the bay.

This computer simulation is one of many analytical tools used in a joint study by Rand and the Netherlands government, which has had important short- and long-term effects. In February 1953, a severe storm from the North Sea flooded much of the Delta region of the Netherlands, inundating 130,000 hectares and killing several thousand people. After this disaster, the Dutch government decided to increase the region's protection from floods by constructing a system of dams and dikes, called the Delta Works, in all the Delta estuaries. By the mid-1970s, this protective construction had been completed, or was well under way, in every Delta estuary except the largest—the Oosterschelde—where construction work had barely begun before it was interrupted by controversy.

The original plan for protecting the Oosterschelde had been to construct an impermeable dam across the nearly 9-kilometer-wide

---

[5] S. S. Leendertse and D. S. K. Liu, *A Water-Quality Simulation Model for Well Mixed Estuaries and Coastal Seas, Vol. 8, An Engineering Assessment.* Rand Report R-1791-NYC (Santa Monica, Calif.: The Rand Corporation, December 1975). See also *Final Report, 1969–1976,* pp. 21–22, 64–65.

mouth of the estuary, thereby closing off the estuary from the sea, and then to turn the resulting basin into a fresh-water lake. This, however, threatened the Oosterschelde's extremely rich and rare ecology and its thriving oyster and mussel fishing industry.

In 1974, in response to the growing controversy, the Dutch cabinet directed the Rijkwaterstaat, the government agency responsible for water control and public works, to study an alternative approach: the construction in the mouth of the Oosterschelde of a special kind of dam called a storm-surge barrier. Basically, the storm-surge barrier would be a flow-through dam containing many large gates. In a severe storm, these gates would be closed; under normal conditions, they would be open to allow a reduced tide—somewhat smaller than the original—to pass into the Oosterschelde basin from the sea.

Some opponents of the original plan were fearful that the storm-surge barrier, with its reduced tide, might seriously damage the fishing or the ecology. They pressed for yet another alternative: a plan where the mouth of the Oosterschelde would be left open to maintain the original tide and a system of large dikes to protect the land would be built in place of the existing dikes around its perimeter.

It soon became clear that the process of comparison and choice among the Oosterschelde alternatives would be very difficult, for their potential consequences were many, varied, and hard to assess. To aid the decision-making process, a joint project was set up in 1975 between Rand and the Rijkswaterstaat.

For the alternative cases, the project team analyzed and compared many different consequences, in a variety of categories: the security of people and property from flooding; the financial costs to the government of the construction and operation of the works; the changes in the kind and populations of species that form the ecology of the region; the additional employment and other economic effects that occur not only in industries directly involved in the construction of the barrier but also in interrelated industries; the quantity and quality of the water supply available in various locations; and the many social effects, including the displacement of households and the possibly disproportionate effects on the various regions and sectors of the economy.

In April 1976 Rand presented its work to the Rijkswaterstaat, describing the methodological framework that had been developed and summarizing the results of the analysis. The Rijkswaterstaat combined this work with several special studies of its own and submitted its report to the Cabinet, which discussed each policy alternative, measured its impact on each of many factors, and recommended the storm-surge barrier plan to Parliament. Parliament voted to accept the recommended option in June 1976, and detailed engineering studies and implementation are now well underway.

**California Energy Study.** A third example of intermediate-term direct impact on a crucial area of policy at the state level promises also to have considerable effect over the long run. Responding to the needs of the Committee on Planning and Land Use of the California State Assembly, and as part of a program of energy policy studies that had begun in the late 1960s, Rand conducted a series of policy analyses on the rate of growth in demand for electrical energy, the need to reduce that rate of growth, ways and means by which conservation measures might slow the rate of growth, and evaluation of the side-effects of a slowed growth rate.[6] Rand also examined and evaluated alternative options for siting power plants in the state and studied the need for a power-plant siting agency. Out of this work grew legislation establishing the California Energy Resources Conservation and Development Commission, which was responsible for "demand management" within the state—providing for the first time an independent commission to assess the demand projections of the utilities, to analyze needs for new power-plant construction so as to meet projected demand, to deal with issues of power-plant siting, and to conduct a program of research and development on new energy technologies. While helping to establish a new independent commission within state government may or may not be a good thing per se, it is evidence of the positive impact of policy analysis in establishing through legislation a body responsible for query and review of state energy demand estimates and for reporting systematically to the governor and the public its overall assessment of California's energy problems and needs. In fact, the Commission is conducting a series of hearings throughout the state to gather ideas and criticisms from the general public and is also soliciting such inputs by mail and telephone. The work of the Commission is expected to contribute significantly to state energy policy over the long run.

**Firefighting.** Finally, an example of the early, ongoing, and continuing impact of policy analysis on one part of a major problem—firefighting—also illustrates the role policy analysis can play in an area in which there has been scant basic research. Little is known about the causes and prevention of fire or about the damage fire does to

---

[6] W. R. Ahern et al., *Energy Alternatives for California: Paths to the Future: Executive Summary*, Rand Report R-1793/1-CSA/RF (Santa Monica, Calif.: The Rand Corporation, December 1975).

society. Not only are there a lot of questions to which the answers are not known, but the policy analyst can also make a major contribution by discovering the right questions to ask about firefighting.

The United States record in firefighting is a very poor one. We have higher losses per capita—in deaths and damage—than any other modern industrial society. Whether Americans really start more fires than other people, accidentally and on purpose, or whether we simply do a better job of reporting and keeping records is unknown. Nor do we know whether this difference between Americans and others comes from our national attitude of a "throwaway culture," or from our different concepts of legal liability, or from some other factor.

We try to minimize fire damage by fire prevention campaigns, smoke detectors, fire departments, fire insurance, and hospital burn clinics. But we do not know what the effects would be of different arrangements, different levels of effort, or different allocations of effort to these various activities.

While national energy policy is much in the minds of all of us, little thought has been given to the relative fire hazards of competing fuels, the costs of those hazards and the costs of minimizing them, the fire risks of alternative distribution processes (pipelines or rail links, for example), and so on. Likewise, a great deal of effort goes into building codes, their detailed formulation and local enforcement. But no one knows whether all this has much effect on fire safety. We do not know whether authority should continue to be vested at the local level or should be moved to the state or federal level. Nor do we know whether it would be better to abandon the existing code system and instead place the burden of fire protection on new insurance provisions.

Fire strikes hardest at the very old, the very young, and the poor. But we do not know what is cause, what effect. Do the young and the elderly start more fires, or are they less able to deal with them? Are some fire problems uniquely associated somehow with the poor, or is it rather that the poor are predominantly old people and children?

The New York City-Rand Institute's work with the New York City Fire Department—one of our most successful analytical collaborations—has also had an effect on firefighting organizations nationwide.[7] Yet today's answers to all the broader questions raised above is still that we do not know. Tomorrow's answers will depend on how much intelligent effort is devoted to them.

---

[7] *Final Report, 1969–1976*, pp. 9–12, 56–59.

## Indirect Effects of Policy Analysis

Among the most specific and immediately identifiable of the indirect effects of policy analysis is the impact of social experimentation on privacy in social science research, on privacy in general, and on the formulation of measures to protect individual rights to privacy in the context of burgeoning government inquiries, information systems, and data banks. Important privacy issues were raised in the New Jersey Experiment, in the Housing Assistance Supply Experiment, in the Health Insurance Study, and in other policy analysis and research activities. In the housing experiment, for example, the resolution of conflicts between the obligations of the General Accounting Office (GAO) to evaluate and audit government programs and the assurances given by Rand that individual privacy would be preserved has thus far clarified a number of issues; it has preserved the rights both of individuals and of the GAO; and it offers promise that the quality of GAO evaluations and audits may improve significantly as the result of a study sponsored by the GAO now being conducted by the Social Science Research Council.

In a more general sense, analytical studies as well as the vast store of information regarding individuals accumulated by various government agencies have generated an increasing (and, in my judgment, proper) concern with the issue of privacy and government policy toward preservation of individual privacy.

The privacy issue received a significant impetus when Secretary Elliot Richardson of the Department of Health, Education, and Welfare chartered a committee to examine the record-keeping practices of his agency. Willis Ware was borrowed from Rand to be chairman of the committee, whose 1973 report, *Records, Computers, and the Rights of Citizens,* has had a profound effect on the privacy issue in this country and, to some extent, in the world.[8] The committee set forth five general principles it regarded as the foundation for privacy safeguards:

1. There must be no personal data record-keeping systems whose very existence is secret.
2. There must be a way for an individual to find out what information about him is in a record and how it is used.
3. There must be a way for an individual to prevent information about him that was obtained for one purpose from

---

[8] U.S. Department of Health, Education, and Welfare, *Records, Computers, and the Rights of Citizens, A Report of the Secretary's Advisory Committee on Automated Personal Data Systems,* DHEW Publication (05) 73-97, July 1973.

being used or made available for other purposes without his consent.

4. There must be a way for an individual to correct or amend a record of identifiable information about him.

5. Any organization creating, maintaining, using, or disseminating records of identifiable personal data must assure the reliability of the data for their intended use and must take precautions to prevent misuse of the data.[9]

The Committee also suggested features that a code of fair information practice might contain.

This report has set the tone for most legislative attempts to treat privacy in an omnibus fashion. For example, the Federal Privacy Act of 1974 is based on the concepts, the principles, and even the language introduced by the HEW report, as are many state efforts. Both the concept of a code of fair information practice and its details are now widely used as the foundation of privacy legislation in the United States, and its applicability is being studied in other countries. Policy analysis and related research on the privacy issues conducted at Rand and elsewhere underlie many aspects of the HEW report. Analysis of how best to extend protection to record-keeping systems maintained by criminal justice and law enforcement agencies of state and local governments, and by private industry, will form an important part of future research.

Other indirect effects of policy analysis, viewed as a new scientific activity, may be found in an observable change in the ways statesmen and bureaucrats alike think about problems, debate among themselves and with each other, and in general set the tone of policy debates. For example, though it would be difficult to define the precise impact of any particular section of the Brookings Institution's "counter-budget" volumes,[10] the overall impact has led government to ask new questions in new ways, to increase the quality and precision of answers demanded, and to develop ways in which answers such as those produced by the Congressional Budget Office and the Office of Management and Budget may be used by official consumers and, in many instances, by the general public.

One can be more precise about the impact of the Office of Technology Assessment's initial evaluation of the work of the Energy Research and Development Administration, for ERDA was quick to respond to the OTA's analysis by making a number of major in-house

---

[9] Ibid., pp. xx–xxi.

[10] *Setting National Priorities* (Washington, D.C.: The Brookings Institution, 1969–1978), annual publication.

changes, the most important of which was a reformulation of its view of its role in the energy policy (as opposed to energy hardware) business. And students of the Center for Technology Assessment and Resource Policy at Stanford are helping bring to bear not only the enthusiasm of their youth but also the latest analytical tools on assignment to various branches and agencies of government, particularly in the area of natural resources management.

It seems to me that a new atmosphere has begun to surround the policy-making process, and that policy analysis has had a major role in its development. This is not to suggest that policy analysis is always right, or that it invariably affects important policy decisions, nor would I argue that it could do so, or, in cases where quality or objectivity of the analysis are of concern, that it should do so. I do argue that policy analysis, in spite of its relative youth as a science and in spite of its sometimes excessive ambitions and its frequent overbilling as a panacea, has had and will continue to have major effects on policy and on the policy process.

## Statesmen and Bureaucrats

What then of the effects of analytical work on statesmen and bureaucrats? Is there some insidious movement underway to arm bureaucratic legions with weapons with which to override the intuitive wisdom of the statesman in his definition of the public interest? Will a pitched battle be joined between the big guns of policy and the "pea-brained dinosaur" of the federal bureaucracy—or of state and local government, or of municipal or private unions—newly equipped with analytical tools designed to swamp statesmanlike decisions with the minutiae of unimportant and irrelevant problems? I believe the answer is "could be, but probably not"; I believe this for several reasons.

First, as I suggested earlier, there are fewer pure statesmen and bureaucrats than one might suppose. Most government officials (and advisors to governments as well) are mixed cases: most successful statesmen know how to play bureaucrat very well indeed; conversely, there are more statesmanlike qualities among senior bureaucrats than some might think. Thus the battle—should one be joined—will be among human beings in positions of responsibility for participating in public decision making; like all of us, their characteristics and goals are often mixed and change over time. Both bureaucrats and statesmen seek knowledge as a basis for their decisions; and both can be informed by policy analysis. Should they fail to agree—or even when they do agree—policy analysis can be critical in defining exactly what the issue is, and the nature of the areas of mutual understanding, agreement, and disagreement.

Second, there are few major issues of domestic social policy today that have not been informed by analytical research: health policy, housing, education, youth and minority labor-market participation, criminal justice, urban policy—all have received careful analytical treatment within the government and by independent institutions such as Rand, Brookings, the Urban Institute, and others. Methods, data, analyses, alternatives—all have been provided to and used by statesmen and bureaucrats, within the limits of their views of feasibility.

Third, policy analysis most often does *not* seek to provide answers to "the health problem," "the crime problem," "the condition of modern American society," "the urban crisis," or other issues that sound so important but are, in the form stated, merely rhetoric. Without denying the rhetorical utility of such problem statements, the policy analyst seeks to define the myriad elements of these problems, and to work systematically at developing alternative courses of action in as many of them as possible, dealing as well as he can with the links and interactions among them. A senior bureaucrat who understands his job will also understand this process; he should, and often does, seek to inform the statesman—the senior decision maker—of the options and their probable consequences as derived from policy analysis. At the same time, of course, the public should have access to this information and should use it not only to judge the congeniality of decisions made in their interest, but also to distinguish the *reasoning* from the *reasons* underlying those decisions.

My point is not, of course, that we have the optimal number of bureaucrats at various levels of government; it is rather that policy analysis can form a crucial substantive link between the bureaucrat and the statesman, increasing the effectiveness of each and the quality of the decision-making process itself.

Finally, with full public disclosure of analysis in the ongoing policy debate, analysis can be an effective means of achieving decisions that reflect not only rationality but also values and beliefs. Among the chief virtues of policy analysis in a pluralistic, democratic society is that it can help all its participants to understand the differences between rational analysis and the process of choosing among alternative courses of action on the basis of values, particular special interests, and political considerations. The bureaucrat and statesman can both conduct and understand policy analyses; ultimately, perhaps policy analysis can help make both accountable to the public interest they have been selected to serve.

# 5

# Congress, Policy Analysis, and Natural Gas Deregulation: A Parable about Fig Leaves

*Michael J. Malbin*

It has been three decades since the Legislative Reorganization Act of 1946 first authorized congressional committees to hire permanent professional staffs. Since then, committee and personal staffs have mushroomed; today they are about six times their original size.

Every time congressional staffs have increased, the publicly stated justification has been the same: Congress needs its own sources of information if it is to remain independent of the executive branch and of private interest groups.

Over the years, this justification became almost ritualized, even as the staffs became steadily more partisan and less purely informational. But in 1970 it took an interesting turn. Although the Legislative Reorganization Act of 1970 spurred a new spurt in growth, it also required the Congressional Research Service and the General Accounting Office to move beyond their traditional functions, reference and audit, to a new function: providing Congress with "policy analysis." The 1972 act creating the new Office of Technology Assessment, and the Budget Impoundment and Control Act of 1974 creating the Congressional Budget Office, gave those two new agencies similar mandates.

Congress's new interest in policy analysis can be traced to at least three causes: its growing acceptance in academia; desire of congressional Democrats to have analysts of "their own" to counter material produced by the Nixon administration; and a sense of caution induced by the mixed performance of Great Society programs. The

This essay is adapted from a chapter in the author's forthcoming book, *Unelected Representatives: Congressional Staffs and the Future of Representative Democracy*, to be published in New York by Basic Books. Copyright 1980 by Michael J. Malbin.

result was major growth not only in the number of support agency professionals but also in the number of House and Senate staff members with advanced professional degrees.

What all this staff growth means for the level of information in Congress depends upon two separate factors: the quality of the analysis itself and the uses to which it is put. Both supporters and critics of policy analysis seem to assume that the increased number of policy analysts on Capitol Hill has meant more influence for their analyses.[1] The assumption has a surface plausibility: Why else keep the analysts around? But the fact that analysis is produced, or even that it is cited in debate, does not mean that it is used *as analysis*. We all know, for example, that there is a great deal of difference between the ways a scholar and a trial lawyer use material provided by experts. One wants a reasoned argument, the other needs ammunition. To know how Congress uses this ever-increasing supply of analysis, therefore, one must look at the ultimate point of consumption—at the way members themselves use and understand the material they cite in the course of their deliberations.

A quick overview of the situation provides support for both the analytic and the cynical view of the way members use the material they cite. The cynical view—by far the more common one in Washington—gains support from the fact that some 45 percent of committee staff professionals hold law degrees and only about 8 percent hold Ph.D.'s.[2] The percentage of Ph.D.'s is not insignificant, but their work almost always is filtered through staff directors and members of Congress, whose professional training leads them to think in adversary terms.

On the other hand, some analyses have had direct and at least occasionally beneficial effects on the legislative process. For example, the original Humphrey-Hawkins full employment bill, calling for the politically attractive goal of 3 percent employment by 1980, seemed all but assured of passage in 1976 until Charles Schultze, then of the Brookings Institution, pointed out that its goal would be impossible to achieve without other economic dislocations Congress was not likely to support.[3] Perhaps more to the point, the failure of the admin-

---

[1] For a critic who makes this connection, see Edward Banfield, in this volume.

[2] Harrison W. Fox, Jr., and Susan Webb Hammond, *Congressional Staffs: The Invisible Force in American Lawmaking* (New York: Free Press, 1977), p. 175. Fox's and Hammond's numbers are based on 1972 surveys. The percentage of both attorneys and Ph.D.'s probably is higher today.

[3] James W. Singer, "The Humphrey-Hawkins Bill—Boondoggle or Economic Blessing?" *National Journal*, June 12, 1976, pp. 812–15.

istration's welfare reform package in 1978 can be attributed in part to a Congressional Budget Office analysis of its costs.[4]

In other words, the role of policy analysis in congressional deliberation may be both more complex and more ambiguous than most observers realize. Perhaps we should avoid generalizations, therefore, and look at a specific case in which members of Congress made extensive references to analyses in the course of their debates. Conclusions from a single case study may or may not carry over to others, but at least they have the advantage of beginning from direct observation.

## Natural Gas Pricing

The 1977–1978 debate over natural gas pricing is a good example of how Congress uses policy analysis. It was chosen for two reasons. First, the cost to consumers of alternative natural gas pricing schemes and the effect of prices on supplies were studied extensively by economists inside and outside the legislative branch. Each of the four congressional support agencies contributed important material. The principal economic study used by House Democrats was produced by a subcommittee staff professional, and the principal counterstudy was done by a freshman Republican member who previously had been a congressional staff aide. These legislative studies all but dominated the 1977 floor debate, displacing the material produced by the administration, on one side, and industry trade associations, on the other.

The second reason is less straightforward. President Carter and the leaders of Congress concurred in giving the president's energy package the top legislative priority of 1977–1978, and they acknowledged beforehand that natural gas pricing would be the package's most divisive issue. This visibility clearly increased the supply of information available. Although normally the four support agencies have an elaborate system for avoiding duplication in their research efforts, all four produced analyses of the president's energy plan, each contributing something distinctive to the debate. If ever there were an issue in which the size of congressional staffs affected the information available to members, this was it.

Yet the reams of econometric analysis on natural gas did little more than divert Congress from the issues that should have been

---

[4] For an article on the analyses of welfare reform, see Linda E. Demkovich, "The Numbers Are the Issue in the Debate over Welfare Reform," *National Journal*, April 22, 1978, pp. 633–37.

addressed—the ones underlying the analyses. The reasons for Congress's failure to recognize the connection between assumptions and conclusions in these studies do not apply only to the natural gas controversy; they are the same factors that keep Congress generally from being an intelligent user of analysis, able to sift the good from the bad. Members are simply too busy and insufficiently knowledgeable to do that sifting. Hence, they are persuaded of or cynical about particular pieces of analysis for reasons that often have little to do with the merits of the study in question. Instead, they have to fall back, intuitively, on something they rely on in most of what they do. Unable to judge the substance, members judge people. They rely on their sense of a particular analyst's trustworthiness and (depending on which is wanted) objectivity or political loyalty.

Some of the gas studies used in 1977 were better than others, of course, while some very good ones were not used at all in the congressional debate. The following review is limited to the material actually used by Congress in the 1977 floor debates and the marathon 1977–1978 natural gas conference. Although this analysis may contain more information about natural gas pricing than many readers ever wanted to know, it is only through such a detailed examination that a central truth can emerge: the policy analyses in question were based on assumptions that predetermined their conclusions.

## Historical Background

To understand the 1977–1978 deregulation debate, we must go back to 1954, when the Federal Power Commission (FPC) was told by the Supreme Court[5] to regulate the wellhead price of natural gas destined for the interstate market.[6] Since most natural gas at the time was a waste byproduct from oil well drilling, gas prices were quite low—about $0.18 per thousand cubic feet (mcf) in 1959. This price stayed virtually unchanged through the 1960s. Natural gas production increased from 4 trillion cubic feet (tcf) in 1945 to 13 tcf in 1960 and 22 tcf in 1970.

---

[5] Phillips Petroleum Co. v. Wisconsin, 347 U.S. 672 (1954).
[6] The material in this historical overview is based largely on Paul W. MacAvoy and Robert S. Pindyck, *Price Controls and the Natural Gas Shortage* (Washington, D.C.: American Enterprise Institute, 1975), pp. 11–16; Robert S. Pindyck, "Prices and Shortages: Evaluating Policy Options for the Natural Gas Industry" in Albert Carnesale et al., *Options for U.S. Energy Policy* (San Francisco: Institute for Contemporary Studies, 1977), pp. 143–77; and Edmund W. Kitch, "Regulation of the Field Market for Natural Gas by the Federal Power Commission," *Journal of Law and Economics*, vol. 11 (October 1968), pp. 243–80.

The 1970s saw a decline in production and an increase in the regulated wellhead price of new natural gas. By 1972, the average area rate for new contracts was about $0.34/mcf. In 1975 the FPC announced its first uniform national rate, $0.42/mcf; by June 1976 this had risen to $1.42. The price increases did not forestall production shortages, however. With demand increasing at an annual rate of about 5 percent, production fell from 22.6 tcf in 1973 to 19.5 tcf in 1976. Proven gas reserves dropped from 292 tcf in 1967 to 216 tcf in 1976, about an eleven-year supply at current rates of consumption.[7]

As production has declined, the gas industry has argued that the best way to get it back up again would be to end price regulation and let prices rise to market levels, thus offsetting the high costs of drilling and exploration. Industry critics reply that prices were allowed to increase in the 1970s with no increase in supply. The industry answers that none of the price increases amounted to much until 1976, and drilling has increased markedly since then.

President Carter's National Energy Plan, announced April 20, 1977, partially accepted the gas industry's view that the price for new gas should be higher than the price allowed by the FPC in 1976. The administration called for a new-gas price of $1.75/mcf that would increase with the consumer price index. The plan also would have applied federal price regulations for the first time to gas produced and sold within the same state, ending the dual interstate-intrastate gas market. The administration's price—higher than the FPC's but lower than the anticipated deregulated price—thus would have meant an increase in the price of gas sold on the interstate market and a decrease in the intrastate gas price.

Just as the administration's proposals of 1977–1978 represented an attempt to go part way toward satisfying advocates of deregulation, so the deregulation proposals offered in Congress in 1977–1978 went part way toward meeting the fears of those worried about the immediate impact of a sudden price increase on consumers. All recent deregulation amendments with a serious chance of passing have cushioned the impact on consumers by limiting deregulation to newly discovered gas. Since most gas purchased at any one time is covered by existing contracts, this limitation meant that higher deregulated prices would be introduced gradually.

The 1977 bills also contained another consumer cushion: incremental pricing. Developed in 1974 by Leslie J. Goldman, then an aide

---

[7] For the production and reserve figures, see: U.S. Congress, Joint Economic Committee, *The Economics of the Natural Gas Controversy*, staff study, 95th Cong., 1st sess., Sept. 19, 1977, pp. 14 and 22.

to Sen. Adlai E. Stevenson III (Democrat, Illinois), incremental pricing was designed to require industrial users of natural gas to bear the full cost of any increase in new-gas prices before any of that cost was averaged into the price paid by residential users. The purpose of this was to spread the burden of a price increase to all consumers (purchasers of industrial goods) before letting it fall disproportionally on people heating their homes with gas. This concept was embodied in different forms in both the administration's and the Senate's bills in 1977, and it became an important focal point for bargaining during the 1977–1978 conference.

The issue of gas pricing divided the House and Senate fairly evenly in 1977, with different results in the two chambers. Deregulation was defeated in the House on August 3, 1977, by a vote of 199-227, twenty-four votes more than the 1976 margin. The Senate had to break a two-week filibuster-by-amendment before accepting deregulation on October 4. The key vote, coming on September 22, was 52-46 for deregulation.

An incredible number of econometric studies were cited in the 1977 natural gas pricing debate. One reason for this was that in 1977, as in earlier years, members of Congress saw the impact of gas prices on gas supplies and consumer costs as the prime issue in the debate. Everyone agreed that deregulation eventually would mean higher home heating prices and that this would create at least some hardship for people on fixed incomes—the question was, how much of a hardship and to what avail? If deregulation would mean increased supplies (and, therefore, lessened dependence on foreign fuel and a more productive national industrial capacity) at a modest increase in consumer costs, that would lead to one political conclusion. If, on the other hand, it would mean sharply higher energy costs for consumers, little increase in supplies, higher-priced manufactured goods, and a worsening trade deficit (as we imported the same amount of oil while the price of manufactured goods put them at a competitive disadvantage), that would lead to quite a different political conclusion. As a result, politicians who asked about costs and supplies before they voted were asking an important question. Economists familiar with the subject recognized its importance and churned out numerous "answers."

While many studies were cited in the floor debates of 1977, a few stood out from the rest. House supporters of the administration's position relied primarily on an analysis produced by the staff of the House Interstate and Foreign Commerce Committee's Subcommittee on Energy and Power, chaired by Rep. John Dingell (Democrat, Michigan).[8] Deregulation advocates in the House relied on work done by a freshman member of the subcommittee, Rep. David Stockman (Republican, Michigan), for himself and the subcommittee's ranking Republican, Clarence (Bud) Brown of Ohio.[9]

In the Senate, administration supporters, led by Sen. Henry Jackson of Washington, relied on a study done for him by the Congressional Budget Office.[10] Critics of the administration from a pro-consumer perspective, such as Edward M. Kennedy (Democrat, Massachusetts), Howard Metzenbaum (Democrat, Ohio), and James Abourezk (Democrat, South Dakota), generally cited a study done by Lawrence Kumins of the Congressional Research Service for the Joint Economic Committee.[11] Supporters of deregulation, such as James Pearson (Republican, Kansas) and Lloyd Bentsen (Democrat, Texas), used a study done by Edward W. Erickson for the Natural Gas Supply Committee, an industry group.[12] A General Accounting Office study, which took no position on the merits of deregulation, was cited by people on all sides of the issue.[13]

## Against Deregulation: The Administration

The administration's own studies were conspicuously given short shrift in the 1977 floor debates. The White House Energy Policy and Planning Office, headed by James R. Schlesinger, was responsible for the president's energy package until the Department of Energy opened for business on October 1, 1977. Schlesinger's office produced quantitative analyses of the impact of deregulation that were every

---

[8] U.S. Congress, House of Representatives, Committee on Interstate and Foreign Commerce, *National Energy Act*, Report Together with Minority, Additional, and Supplemental Views (to accompany H.R. 6831), H. Rept. 95-496, pt. 4, 95th Cong., 1st sess., July 19, 1977, pp. 85–124.

[9] Ibid., pp. 313–29.

[10] U.S. Congressional Budget Office, *Natural Gas Pricing Proposals: A Comparative Analysis*, printed at the request of Senator Henry M. Jackson, Chairman, U.S. Senate Committee on Energy and Natural Resources, Publication 95-50, September 1977. Cited by Senator Jackson in floor debate, Sept. 19, 1977. *Congressional Record*, daily edition, S15149. At least fourteen other Senators referred to this study in the course of the Senate debate.

[11] U.S. Congress, Joint Economic Committee, staff study prepared for the use of the Subcommittee on Energy, *The Economics of the Natural Gas Controversy*, 95th Cong., 1st sess., Sept. 19, 1977.

[12] Natural Gas Supply Committee, *The Net Benefits to the American Economy of Deregulation of the Price of New Natural Gas* (Washington, D.C.: September 1977).

[13] Comptroller General of the United States, *An Evaluation of the National Energy Plan*, Report to the Congress, July 25, 1977, EMD-77-48.

bit as detailed as the ones done by Dingell's staff and by the congressional support agencies. White House press aides gave the office's numbers wide currency in the weeks before floor debate when they told reporters that deregulation would be a "$70-billion rip-off" of the American consumer.[14] Nevertheless, the administration's numbers were cited rarely in floor debate, for two reasons. First, members of Congress prefer to use their own material when they can. Second, and more importantly, the administration's methodology was seen to be biased and simplistic.

The administration's studies of natural gas deregulation were released in May 1977. According to the White House Energy Policy and Planning Office, President Carter's proposal to increase the regulated price of natural gas from $1.42/mcf to $1.75/mcf while imposing controls on the unregulated intrastate market would result in almost as much of an increase in supply as would occur under deregulation. Costs, on the other hand, would be substantially lower under the president's plan, because $1.75 would be a high enough price to encourage suppliers to tap most known or probable resources. Allowing the price to go higher would only result in the development of smaller, less productive wells at too high a marginal cost.

Since the administration assumed that natural gas prices above $1.75 would have little or no impact on supplies, its notion of distributive equity governed its attitude toward prices above $1.75. The administration feared that without regulation, consumers would bid prices up, yielding economic "rents" to the producers. Since the producers would and could do nothing in return, Schlesinger and his colleagues felt it appropriate to refer to any earnings they might receive as unjust.[15]

Schlesinger's views about equity were common among supporters of continued regulation, but the way the administration figured costs was unique. The administration presented four possible scenarios or cases for deregulation, each one assuming that all uncom-

---

[14] President Carter never used the phrase "$70-billion rip-off" himself, but he did refer to a $70-billion cost at a September 29, 1977, press conference during the Senate anti-deregulation filibuster, and he used the word "rip-off" in an October 13, 1977, press conference. The full phrase was used by many others in the administration, however. See *Congressional Quarterly Weekly*, March 18, 1978, p. 713, for Carter's varied statements on deregulation.

[15] In fact, when Representative Stockman tried to get Schlesinger to say the administration had resource goals in mind as well as distributive justice, Schlesinger resisted. See U.S. Congress, House of Representatives, Subcommittee on Energy and Power of the Committee on Interstate and Foreign Commerce, Hearings on *The National Energy Act*, pt. 2, Natural Gas, 95th Cong., 1st sess., May 12, 13, 17, and 18, 1977, Serial 95-23, p. 242.

mitted gas would be decontrolled immediately.[16] This was an accurate reflection of what the industry wanted, but it was not what Congress was considering. The bills adopted by the Senate and narrowly defeated in the House compromised deregulation with incremental pricing, transitional controls over offshore gas until 1982, and more stringent definitions of "new" or "uncommitted" gas than the administration analysis assumed. Undaunted by this discrepancy, the administration concluded that proposed deregulation measures would produce revenues "somewhere between those of the first and third cases." How this assertion was justified remains unclear to this day, but it was the source of the "$70-billion rip-off" charge. The one figure in the administration analyses fitting that description was the one for the second case: 1978–1985 producer revenues of $86 billion more than under existing law (called the *base case* by the administration). Subtract the $15 billion producers supposedly would get under the president's bill from $86 billion, and one is left with $71 billion.

All the administration's cost estimates were based ultimately on its estimate of the cost of continuing as is, without changing the law. Unfortunately for its future political credibility, the administration misread this base case very seriously. The errors were first spotted by an aide to Rep. Robert Krueger (Democrat, Texas), a supporter of deregulation, and were confirmed by Walter W. (Chip) Schroeder, an economic modeling specialist on Representative Dingell's subcommittee staff. In a note Schroeder wrote to Krueger, Schroeder said the administration's base case assumed that gas on the unregulated intrastate market would sell for $0.62/mcf in 1978 and $0.70/mcf in 1985. These estimates were far too low, he continued: subcommittee testimony indicated that average intrastate prices in 1977 already were in the $1.30 to $1.35 range. Schroeder wrote in the note, "If one assumes a 1978 price of $1.35 and a 1985 price of $2.40 (still below the distillate equivalent price), then the administration analysis understates producer revenues under continued regulation by $4.53 billion in 1978 and a cumulative total of $44.36 billion through 1985. This means that case 1 deregulation costs $56 billion minus $44 billion, or $12 billion." Schroeder's own analysis, based on different assumptions, put the cost of deregulation much higher than this. But

---

[16] "Producer Revenues and Consumer Costs under Decontrol," released May 1977 by the White House Energy Policy and Planning Office, Natural Gas Task Force. This paper was reprinted in: U.S. Congress, Senate, Committee on Energy and Natural Resources, Hearings on *Natural Gas Pricing Proposals of President Carter's Energy Program* (Part D of S. 1469), 95th Cong., 1st sess., June 7, 13, 14, and 17, 1977, publication 95-75.

his weakening of the administration's assumptions punctured one of its key arguments: that the National Energy Plan was a compromise between present law and deregulation from the producer's point of view. Instead, it appeared that the administration bill would mean significantly lower revenues for producers than the status quo.

This put the administration in a political box. When its gas pricing proposal was defeated in the Senate after winning narrowly in the House, it became clear that the administration would have to come closer to the industry's position if it wanted a compromise. However, every time it tried that, it faced the prospect of losing some of its original support from people who accepted its original claim that keeping the status quo was best. If it had acknowledged its original errors openly and promptly, the administration still might have been able to play the role of honest broker. Instead, its handling of the technical data throughout 1977 and 1978 aroused suspicions in Congress that the administration was trying to mislead them. Instead of helping the deliberative process, the administration's analysis was part of the political problem the administration had to overcome before it could get Congress to agree on anything.

The administration's "base case" numbers clearly were causing problems in the early months of the marathon energy conference, when each side considered the status quo better for its position than compromise. One compromise proposal, which looked a good deal like the one that later was adopted, was soundly defeated by Senate conferees in December. (Senator Jackson labelled the proposal a "Christmas turkey.") The administration then decided—finally—to jettison its original numbers. Over the Christmas recess, Secretary Schlesinger and other Department of Energy officials visited Senator Jackson and tried to convince him that a deadlock, continuing the status quo, could be a lot worse for the consumer than he realized. The department had just completed a review of its base case figures and decided it had underestimated the cost of the status quo by almost $20 billion. Jackson was not convinced immediately. Skeptical of economic models in general, and aware of the criticism of this model in particular, he wanted to make sure this was not just another politicized analysis designed to fit the administration's desire for a bill. Only after Jackson confirmed the new data with Schroeder did the conference make its first glacial movements toward the compromise bill that was finally adopted.

The situation just described is a good illustration of why Congress feels it needs professionals of its own. If the analysts do no more than free members of Congress from their dependency on politicized, or intellectually sloppy, administration analysis, that is no small benefit. Whether Congress's own analyses affirmatively helped the debate is another question, to which we now turn.

## Against Deregulation: The Energy and Power Subcommittee

The two most widely used studies on the administration's side of the deregulation debate were those produced by Representative Dingell's Energy and Power Subcommittee and by the Congressional Budget Office (CBO).

The econometric model the Energy and Power Subcommittee used for its analyses was designed by Chip Schroeder. Schroeder's technical background convinced him during 1975 that the econometric model the administration was using was fundamentally unsound, and he convinced others on Capitol Hill of this conclusion. By early 1976 he had developed a model of his own. Unlike the others then in use, Schroeder's model could analyze the cost of some compromises that might resolve the regulation-deregulation debate, partly because it could predict direct consumer costs for residential users of natural gas, taking account of incremental pricing. In 1977, Schroeder used his model to estimate probable gas supplies and costs under the House version of the administration proposal and six different deregulation scenarios, three of which were close approximations of bills actively being considered by Congress.[17]

Under the three realistic scenarios, Schroeder saw deregulation costing consumers $51.8–53.7 billion more than the House bill for the years 1977–1985, with the major cost being felt in the first five years. After that, new-gas prices under the administration's bill would not differ greatly from those under the deregulation proposals passed by the Senate and defeated by the House, as new-gas prices dropped from $5 back toward the average price for an equivalent amount of energy from oil. (This conclusion lay behind the energy conferees' decision to deregulate all new gas discovered after April 20, 1977, only after continuing regulation through 1985.)

The assumption that the price for deregulated gas initially would soar up to the $5/mcf price range—well above heating oil prices, and well above the administration's assumed figure—is controversial. If this proved not to be the case, Schroeder's overall estimates would

---

[17] House Subcommittee on Energy and Power of the Committee on Interstate and Foreign Commerce, Hearings on *The National Energy Act*, pt. 2, pp. 85–124; U.S. House of Representatives, Subcommittee on Energy and Power of the Committee on Interstate and Foreign Commerce, *Economic Analysis of Natural Gas Policy Alternatives*, December 1977, Subcommittee Print, Committee Print 95-31.

have to be scaled down dramatically. Whether or not short-term gas prices would jump this way depends on two factors that cannot be handled quantitatively by Schroeder's or any other econometric model: the relative balance of short-term supply and demand, and the relative concentration of power among sellers and buyers. Econometric models can build in assumptions about these factors, but they cannot analyze them.

Moving away from the short term, the major long-term dispute relating to Schroeder's work also has to do with supplies. Schroeder, like the administration, believed that deregulating the price of new gas would produce virtually no new gas that would not have been produced with a $1.75 regulated ceiling. For higher prices to produce more supplies, the gas would have to be available in forms that become steadily more recoverable, in economic terms, as the price goes up. A lack of response of supply to price means one of two things: either the resource must be on the verge of exhaustion, or there must be something about the underlying geology of gas to explain the situation.

The relationship between price and supply, which in turn depends on the geophysical characteristics of gas fields and reservoirs, turns out to be the key premise on which any conclusion about the long-term "cost" of deregulation must rest. The relationship normally is expressed quantitatively by economists in terms of a *supply elasticity index*. That index is an expression of the percentage change in supply brought about by a given percentage change in price. If a 100 percent increase in price would double the supply of any given commodity, the supply elasticity index for that commodity would be 1.0. If the same 100 percent increase in price would increase supplies by only 10 percent, the index would be 0.1.

Much of the difference between the administration's supporters and the supporters of deregulation can be understood in terms of their different assumptions about supply elasticity. The administration took the position that the supply elasticity of natural gas was different at different prices. Prices up to $1.75 would bring about a significant response, but above $1.75 the response would drop off to practically nothing. The studies supporting deregulation, in contrast, assumed the supply response to price would remain constant—and substantial—as prices went up.

Schroeder, like the deregulation advocates, used a supply elasticity index that did not change as the price went up, though his was a smaller one (0.1).

Despite his use of a level index for the years 1978–1985, Schroeder endorsed the administration's basic policy conclusion by saying that most of the supply bonus to be gained from deregulation could be achieved if the controlled price were pegged at $1.75 instead of $1.46. His reasoning, however, had little to do with the quantitative assumptions in his econometric model. Schroeder thought producers had been withholding gas from the market because they did not want their new discoveries to be controlled at the old price. He was convinced that as soon as Congress settled with certainty on a new price, whatever it might be, producers would release gas they had been holding.

Schroeder expected little to come from higher prices before 1985 except for the withheld gas. Higher prices probably would stimulate new drilling and lead to new discoveries; however, it usually takes a few years for a new discovery to find its way to market. Therefore, the main supply bonus from higher prices would be likely to occur after the eight-year period (1977–1985) covered by his analysis. Schroeder's decision to cut off his analysis at 1985 is puzzling. By his own account, this means ignoring the main benefits of deregulation while maximizing the costs. Ending the analysis at 1985 may help members of Congress compare closely related compromise alternatives within a time frame to which they can relate politically, but it does seem to bias any effort to think about the fundamental policy questions in the regulation-deregulation debate.

This difficulty is compounded if we start thinking about gas from unconventional sources. One of the industry's arguments for deregulation was that it would give them an incentive to develop technologies for recovering gas from unconventional sources, such as geopressurized methane, Devonian shale, tight formation gas, and the like. Geologists acknowledge that there is much more of this unconventional gas in the earth than there is gas from conventional sources. The question is how to extract it economically.

Schroeder gave two reasons for ignoring unconventional gas in his analysis of deregulation: the technologies were largely hypothetical, and even if they were developed, it appeared unlikely that much unconventional gas would get to market before 1985. While these reasons make sense, they indicate serious conceptual problems with prediction based on quantitative elasticity indexes, whatever the index's size and whoever constructed it. Indexes based on historical performance are an inadequate guide to the future; on the other hand, any effort to get away from historical data necessarily involves highly speculative assumptions which make any resulting numerical index too artificially precise. Perhaps that is why most oil and gas companies have little use for supply elasticity indexes in their internal planning. The seemingly precise indexes, and the cost and supply figures they produce, are conceptual dead ends that beguile members of Congress away from the underlying supply issues they should have been debating.

## Against Deregulation: The Congressional Budget Office

The other important study used on the administration's side was produced by the Congressional Budget Office and cited repeatedly by Senator Jackson in floor debate. As often has been the case in the CBO's short history, its study, more than any other on either side of the debate, tried to explain and present arguments for its important assumptions in terms the members of Congress would find accessible. It was the only study, for example, that took the reader through all the steps leading from predicted supplies to estimated costs.

The study was clear on all but one point—a point that is crucial for understanding the role of congressional staff policy analysis. CBO Director Alice M. Rivlin ended her preface to the study with a sentence that can be found in just about everything the CBO publishes: "In keeping with the CBO's mandate to provide objective analysis, the paper offers no recommendations."[18] Rivlin's posture was politically understandable, but misleading. The CBO may not come out and say, "Congress should do X," but many of its studies contain statements similar to these from the natural gas pricing study:

> This paper concludes that the size of consumer expenditures at risk under deregulation is large and that the likelihood that increased production will be substantial by 1985 is small. If these findings are right, then the question of natural gas deregulation becomes primarily one of income distribution and, to a lesser extent, one of reducing and reallocating the demand for natural gas in response to higher prices. With regard to income distribution, deregulation would transfer large amounts of money from consumers to producers. Thus a value judgment is necessary regarding whether national goals are better served by the income remaining with consumers or being passed to producers. The money received by producers would flow to government in the form of taxes, to stockholders, and/or be retained and, subsequently, reinvested.
>
> Although the expected higher cost to consumers, as well as the lack of substantial production, arouses considerable skepticism about immediate deregulation, it is attractive in

---

[18] U.S. Congressional Budget Office, *Natural Gas Pricing Proposals: A Comparative Analysis*, p. v.

some respects because it bears the promise of being a simple, sweeping solution to a complex and exasperating problem. There are, however, several alternative remedies, some of which can modify deregulation in a manner that lowers the costs but preserves most of the benefits. These alternatives include incremental pricing, a phase-in of deregulation, alternative price ceilings, and deregulation with a wellhead tax.[19]

As these statements show, the CBO may not have said which of several compromise possibilities it was *for*, but it sure let you know what it was *against*. Fortunately, most members of Congress are familiar enough with official disclaimers to be aware of the implied recommendations in a discussion of "costs" and "benefits"; they recognize a policy conclusion when they see one.

The CBO's premises, reasoning, and conclusions about prices were similar to Schroeder's, with the same strengths and weaknesses. The CBO study estimated that, through 1985, immediate deregulation would bring producers $76 billion more than the administration bill would. Much of this, it said, would stem from a rapid surge in the price of deregulated gas to about $4/mcf. This price would go down to about $2.80/mcf by 1985.

The CBO's supply estimates, however, were not based on necessarily imprecise supply elasticity assumptions. Instead, they were based on drilling rates, a figure that is related to, but easier to handle than, elasticity. Unlike the other studies, the CBO's contained a clear statement of its reasoning on this question. The CBO study assumed that higher prices would stimulate drilling—specifically, that the rate of drilling would increase 5.5 percent more quickly per year under the administration plan than under a continuation of present policy. Deregulation, the study assumed, would boost drilling growth by 9 percent more per year. Next, the CBO study assumed a constant rate of discovery for each exploratory foot drilled. (The rate of discovery actually has been declining in recent years, so this probably was an overestimate.) From these two assumptions, the study concluded that deregulation would result in total production of about 19.8 tcf in 1985, compared to 18.9 tcf under the administration plan.

The CBO's assumptions about drilling rates obviously were crucial to its conclusion about the costs and benefits of immediate deregulation. CBO analyst Lawrence Oppenheimer, who did most of the work on gas for the study, said the assumption of a 9 percent annual increase in drilling under deregulation was an optimistic con-

---

[19] Ibid., pp. xi–xii.

sensus estimate from people in the industry. His estimate of a 5.5 percent annual increase under the administration plan was shakier, he acknowledged. It was based on his view that the proposal would decrease drilling incentives in the less productive onshore fields, where new finds are committed now to the intrastate market, while increasing incentives to develop more productive offshore fields.

These assumptions and conclusions reflect some of the same problems as Schroeder's analysis. First, Oppenheimer ignored unconventional gas because his analysis went only through 1985. Second, he has acknowledged that 5.5 percent—and consequently $76 billion—were rough estimates. Yet all through the 1977 floor debate, Jackson and others used the $76 billion figure without qualification, ignoring the more fundamental and more uncertain supply issues. Furthermore, they used the figure as a bludgeon against an amendment to which it did not apply. Oppenheimer was careful to state that the deregulation to which he was referring did not include incremental pricing or any other compromises with immediate deregulation, many of which were included in the actual deregulation provision against which Jackson used the figure.

Some of the CBO analysts are aware of the false impressions their seemingly precise numbers have created, but they do not feel they are in a position to correct the situation. One person at the CBO (who asked not to be identified) described a situation that illustrates the problem. After the outline of the conference report became known, Edmund Muskie, chairman of the Senate Budget Committee, asked the CBO to prepare a memorandum analyzing the compromise. The initial draft response was not quantitative: it described in words and in rough percentage terms how the compromise would stimulate production and increase costs. This draft was rejected within the CBO; some people there thought members of Congress would not pay attention to an analysis without numbers. So, the memo was redrafted to make its rhetorical point quantitative, even though the numbers were more misleading than the words they replaced. (Muskie, incidentally, was persuaded to support the compromise, a decision swaying other liberals who had been thinking of opposing the compromise.)

### For Deregulation: Brown-Stockman

The quantitative studies favoring deregulation were no less problematic than those on the administration's side of the debate. They were intended primarily as ammunition for the deregulation forces. Still, if read carefully, they may sharpen our understanding of the dispute, which is depicted more clearly in the assumptions behind the studies than in their conclusions.

The study done by Rep. David Stockman (Republican, Michigan) for himself and Rep. Clarence Brown (Republican, Ohio), both members of the Subcommittee on Energy and Power, was the most widely used study on the deregulation side of the House debate. In an interview with the author, Stockman was candid about why he did the study: "I started to look at the administration's numbers and realized how phony they were and that motivated me to a counter-study. It seemed better to have a study of our own instead of just taking pot shots at theirs. We only had about one and a half or two weeks before markup to do the job, so there was no time to farm it out. I basically did it at my desk with my hand calculator."

Since the purpose of the study was to counter another study, it is not surprising that this one did no better than the original at examining basic assumptions. The crucial first assumption for Stockman, as for the administration, concerned the amount of gas that would be produced under deregulation. Like the administration, he did not begin from a straight geological assessment of supplies. Instead Stockman simply rejected the administration's thesis that supply elasticity would fall off dramatically as prices went up, and he assumed that the quantitative elasticity index the administration used for prices of $1.45–1.75 would apply for prices above that as well. The assumption was made with literally no analysis of the underlying geology—Stockman might as well have been analyzing soy beans or any other commodity whose supplies are not strongly limited by physical constraints. As in the administration's, Schroeder's, and the CBO's studies, everything else followed from these basic assumptions about the supply elasticity of the resource base.

Stockman predicted that 207.4 tcf of natural gas would be produced from 1978 through 1990 if present policies were to remain unchanged, 214.0 tcf if the House (administration) bill were passed, and 238.8 tcf if new-gas prices were deregulated. The cumulative wellhead cost of the gas through 1990 would be $207.0 billion under the status quo, $249.7 billion under the House bill, and $414.2 billion under deregulation. But for Stockman this was only the beginning of the analysis. Instead of concluding that this difference of $164.5 billion between the House bill and deregulation would be the "cost" of deregulation through 1990, he added all the indirect costs of regulation coming from lower supplies before totaling the bill. The result was dramatic. Instead of deregulation's costing $164.5 billion, Stockman's study concluded it would *save* $47.2 billion—more than a $200-billion turnaround!

The elements that went into this accounting were almost mirror images of the ones that went into the studies on the other side. For example, the price of deregulated new gas was figured at $2.50 in 1978, rising gradually to $2.99 (in constant 1975 dollars) by 1990. Stockman rejected Schroeder's argument that new-gas prices would shoot well above $2.50, asserting that the new gas would get tied up in long-term contracts at lower rates.

On the benefit side of the equation, Stockman estimated that production under deregulation would exceed production under the House bill by about 2 tcf per year in the early 1980s and 3 tcf in the late 1980s. This would be enough of a difference to affect residential users, for whom the substitute fuels are not oil, selling at $2.50 per million Btu, but liquid natural gas, synthetic natural gas, and electricity, the average cost of which was figured at approximately $6 per million Btu. The savings to those who would not have to buy substitute fuels Stockman calculated to be $168 billion. The rest of the savings came from transportation costs: if pipelines carry more gas, their fixed costs can be spread over more units, resulting in lower transportation costs for the end users. This would amount to a $44.2 billion savings from 1978 through 1990. Taken together, transportation and replacement fuel savings more than wipe out the extra wellhead cost of new gas, given Stockman's assumed wellhead price.

It is obvious that Stockman's elasticity assumption was the driving force behind all his other numbers. When he was asked where his assumptions came from, Stockman admitted that he had no idea what the production levels would be under either proposal. "I do happen to know some geology and I believe there are enormous supplies out there," he said. But even if there are not, his views about economics convince him that continued regulation will mean steadily decreasing supplies and that, therefore, deregulation would be the best approach whatever the absolute production levels.

> I don't really know how much conventional natural gas will come from deregulation, but I do know deregulation will give us a more sensible price structure. If supplies are low, prices will go up, and people will switch to more plentiful fuels. From my point of view, I think the economic price structure is just as important as the incremental supplies we might get if we deregulate. The problem is that when we debate natural gas in the Energy and Power Subcommittee, we debate gas in isolation from other fuels or other segments of the economy. The legislative process inevitably separates systemic variables into isolated ones, and whenever that happens, the debate will be phony.

Despite those views, Stockman felt the political realities required a counter-study treating gas as an isolated variable. So he produced one. To do it he had to assume his conclusions about gas supplies, just as his opponents did. Like his opponents, his views on other matters convinced him his assumptions were right. But the "other matters," it will become evident, were really what the debate was about.

## For Deregulation: Erickson

All the other studies used on the deregulation side of the debate were essentially variations on the themes in the Stockman-Brown analysis. The study used most often in the Senate debate was done by Edward W. Erickson, professor of economics and business at North Carolina State University. It was commissioned by the Natural Gas Supply Committee, an industry trade association, and published in September, the same month the bill came up on the Senate floor. Since it was not produced in-house, it will be treated briefly here.

Erickson said the net savings from deregulation would be $123.3 billion through 1990, instead of the $47.2 billion Stockman predicted. Furthermore, Erickson included no transportation savings from increased pipeline use in his September study; his savings all came from the avoidance of expensive replacement fuels. The crucial difference between Erickson's view and Stockman's (or anyone else's) involved his supply assumptions. Erickson's model assumed that the administration bill would depress production levels to 15 tcf per year for 1985–1990, whereas deregulation would increase production to 20 tcf per year over the same period.

Senators who cited Erickson's study in debate used it the same way they used the other studies: they looked for the "bottom line" number in the report ($123.3 billion) and cited it without qualification. No one quoted or even seems to have noticed these sentences: "Too much emphasis should not be placed upon the apparent numerical precision associated with the output of a computer model. A common-sense evaluation of the result is most appropriate." [20] The study also warned the reader, "It is critical that the judgment basis of the Benefit Cost Estimation Model be clearly understood. The Natural Gas Supply Committee does not pretend to have a computer model which will predict to the nearest tenth of a tcf the quantities of natural gas forthcoming under alternative pricing policies." [21]

---

[20] Natural Gas Supply Committee, *The Net Benefits to the American Economy of Deregulation of the Price of New Natural Gas*, p. 59.
[21] Ibid., p. 3.

When asked how his committee concluded that about 20 tcf would be produced under deregulation, Executive Vice-President David H. Foster said the figure was based on an informed intuitive judgment after conversations with people from five of the largest gas-producing companies. Erickson confirmed this, saying that the assumption was "casual, not systematic, but thought out." "What we did," Erickson said, "was ask, 'Suppose we could go back to 20 tcf, what would the effect on the economy be?' Maybe we won't get back to 20 tcf, but if not, whatever causes an erosion under 20 tcf would bring about a similar erosion under the administration bill." Asked how he arrived at 15 tcf for the administration bill, and thus a 5-tcf gap between that bill and deregulation, Erickson said it was based on his view that deregulation would create more incentives than present policy, whereas the administration bill would be a rollback. Thus, Erickson's methodology and quantitative-supply conclusions about the effect of deregulation essentially paralleled the CBO's. The difference between them lay in their analyses of the administration bill. Needless to say, none of the senators citing either of these studies brought this out in the Senate debate.

### The Real Issues

It should be fairly clear by now that all of the seemingly precise numbers on both sides of the deregulation debate rest on intuitive assumptions about production, from which everything else follows. Harrison (Jack) Schmitt (Republican, New Mexico), who had been a Harvard Ph.D., geologist, and astronaut before becoming a freshman senator, was one of the very few members of Congress to address this point. Schmitt noted in Senate debate that natural gas resources, considered apart from the economics of production, exist in quantities that for practical purposes can be considered infinite.[22]

This point is not in dispute. All estimates of potentially recoverable conventional gas reserves indicate from thirty-three to seventy years' worth (750–1500 tcf) of gas in the ground. These estimates refer to reserves in soft rock, recoverable at a profit, with known or foreseeable technologies. Predictions about oil and gas reserves made over the past seventy-five years have consistently been far too pessimistic. Furthermore, none of the estimates include gas from Devonian shale (perhaps another 600 tcf), Rocky Mountain tight formation gas (another 600 tcf), geopressurized methane (500–1,000 tcf more) or other geopressurized resources (yet another 3,000–50,000

---

[22] *Congressional Record*, daily edition, Sept. 22, 1977, pp. S15328–29 and Oct. 4, 1977, pp. S16319–22.

tcf). These resources, if fully developed, could mean another thousand years of supply![23]

Senator Schmitt suggested that whether these physical resources are turned into recoverable reserves will depend upon four factors: price, technology, geology, and the availability of risk capital. The response of supply to price depends at any given time on each of the other three factors. "The fact is that we do not really know what happens to the supply curve above $1.45 mcf," Schmitt said.[24]

The world, in other words, is an uncertain place. To cite an example: in the early 1970s, the federal government sold an extraordinarily expensive lease in the Gulf of Mexico to a joint venture that included some of the world's largest oil companies. The companies were eager to go to work because all the available geophysical data suggested this might be one of the biggest finds in the history of the country. The result: eleven dry holes and a loss of about a quarter of a billion dollars.

This costly failure should serve as a warning to people who treat even informed guesses about the earth's subsurface resources as anything other than guesses. If one example does not make the point adequately, anyone in the petroleum industry can recount stories of companies' giving up on an area after drilling thousands of feet, only to have a competitor move in, drill a little deeper, and make a find. (This is how Occidental Petroleum's huge Libyan oil discoveries of the 1960s were made.)

When one considers that estimates of the world's potential resources base are based on information no better than what was available to the oil companies, it becomes clear that all estimates are probabilistic at best. Projecting estimates into a future with changing economic conditions, unknown technologies, and an uncertain international climate is even more problematic. Yet, all econometric studies must do precisely this before they can begin.

None of this settles the deregulation argument, but it does transform it. The real debate over production turns out to be far less precise than the estimates to a tenth of a tcf might suggest. It is, instead, a debate between those on one side who are optimistic about what is economically recoverable under foreseeable technologies, and those on the other, who are pessimistic.

With the issue thus transformed, one is freed from the tyranny of numbers and can begin to see the other political assumptions that

---

[23] The various estimates are collected in the *Congressional Record,* daily edition, Aug. 3, 1977, p. H8400.

[24] Ibid., Oct. 4, 1977, p. S16321.

went into the econometric models. For example, the models all focused on the costs of deregulation to consumers (or on the revenues
it would bring producers), with disagreements coming over how to
define and quantify those costs or benefits. Any study that looks at
consumer costs obviously does so because the person asking for the
study thinks the issue is important. In this case, James Schlesinger
made it clear in the testimony cited earlier that the administration's
main—indeed, sole—reason for keeping regulation was to avoid the
injustice of transferring huge amounts of money from consumers to
producers with little return. This same concern has motivated all the
studies commissioned by liberal Democrats since 1975. Those favoring
deregulation were left in a defensive posture on the question—always
reacting, always working on "counter-studies"—because they did not
share the same ideas about justice. Representative Stockman captured
a widely held alternative view of justice when he said that if production were going to decline, the aim of federal policy should be to
let the market encourage conservation and a smooth transfer to other
fuels by forcing consumers to face the real cost of energy.[25]

A second crucial set of political assumptions underlies all the
econometric studies: whether optimistic or pessimistic in their supply
estimates, the models all assumed a free market. Those who saw the
gas industry as anticompetitive (primarily liberal Democrats) thus
were operating from a premise inconsistent with the models, even
though they probably cited the models' quantitative conclusions more
often than any other single voting bloc. And the political implications
of assuming a free market are vitally important to the deregulation
side of the debate: if the natural-gas industry is an oligopoly in which
a few companies can collude to withhold supplies from the market,
all predictions about deregulation's yielding an upsurge in production
might have to be thrown out the window.

The assumption of a free market also involves less obvious underlying political assumptions. First, all the arguments for deregulation

---

[25] One can go further than this to assert that the different views about fairness that lay
behind the New Deal Democratic–Republican party realignment were the key elements
in the deregulation roll call votes. The usual interpretation is that the issue was a
regional one. However, on the crucial Senate vote on September 22, 1977, twenty-one
states saw their two senators voting on opposite sides of the issue. In four of these,
senators from the same party disagreed. The other seventeen were Democratic-Re-
publican splits. This compares with eight states with senators from different parties
voting together. Six of those eight (Virginia, Arizona, Nebraska, Massachusetts, New
York, and New Jersey) had a senator who often voted with the other party. That leaves
only Texas and Alaska of the eight. One may add Oklahoma and Louisiana to these
as states where producer interests were paramount. Constituencies played an important role in the other states, of course. But Democrats and Republicans generally were
free to define their constituencies in ways that fit their economic and moral outlooks.

assume that selling gas at the market clearing price would produce incentives for reinvestment in gas exploration. The deregulation bills offered did not *require* companies to reinvest, and producers in the past have refused to commit themselves to reinvestment in return for higher prices. Second, the market clearing price for natural gas is assumed to be the Btu-equivalent price of No. 2 oil. This price is set not by the market but by an international cartel. Those advocating deregulation argue that OPEC's oil prices are so high that letting gas sell at the price of oil will produce enough of an incentive for exploration. They may be right, but that economic assumption rests in turn on four political assumptions: (1) that the United States will continue to live with the cartel's price; (2) that the cartel will not revise its prices sharply downward; (3) that a major new producer will not come along—for instance, Mexico—and refuse to join the cartel; and (4) that political instability in the oil-producing states will not blow the cartel apart.

Thus, the models all had to assume answers to questions that were really ones of geology, international relations, antitrust law, and political philosophy. If members of Congress had understood, debated, and at least tentatively answered those questions in their true complexity, they would have had all they needed to decide how to vote—without the models.

## The Limitations of Policy Analyses

It seems unlikely that this conclusion applies only to natural gas deregulation. I would submit that the enterprise of analyzing policy *at its heart* is the art of asking the right questions, and that framing these questions always embodies assumptions that limit political choices. On this level, the essence of policy analysis—not its tools, but its essence—is identical to the art of the politician.

This observation is not an argument against the political use of economics, econometrics, or cost-benefit analysis. It *is* an argument against using them to answer questions outside their competence. It is also an argument against letting "policy analysts," or their politician employers, claim that political questions can be reduced to quantifiable technical ones. Only after the political questions are resolved— or at least exposed and held constant for the sake of analysis—can policy analysis help politicians evaluate programs.

This brings us back to the original questions: Of what use were the natural gas studies, and to what use were they put? To answer this accurately, we first must specify the context. Chip Schroeder's model helped members of Congress in conference compare the relative (not the absolute) costs of various compromise possibilities. Neither his nor any other model, however, led members to address the assumptions that underlay the political choice between regulation and deregulation. As a result, the members misused the studies in two different ways. Some were cynically playing to the press galleries, throwing numbers around but making up their minds on other grounds. Others looked sincerely to the models for answers. Those members who honestly relied on the quantitative studies were misleading themselves, while those who used them cynically were misleading the public. In neither case did the massive staff effort behind the studies serve to clarify the real issues.

Why, then, did representatives and senators use the studies as heavily as they did? Part of it was public relations, but there were two deeper reasons as well. First, some members hid behind the studies: even though they may have made their decisions on other grounds, they felt more comfortable knowing that if something should go wrong, they would be able to say they simply went along with the experts. In this respect, the political use of studies on Capitol Hill is no different from their use anywhere else in government or business.

The second reason is evident from something Representative Stockman said. Asked by this author why he and other members preferred debating the quantitative conclusions of opposed econometric studies to debating the basic assumptions that went into them, Stockman answered, "Nobody wants to say it's all based on a basic value. My position is that the free market does work, but that is a pretty thin fig leaf for something as important as this."

A fig leaf! Members of Congress apparently are *ashamed* to discuss public issues without clutching the numbers provided by economists. In a post-Weberian world, where "facts" and "values" are thought to have distinct cognitive foundations, politicians are embarrassed about basing political choices on principles of justice, or "basic values." Or, they are ashamed to acknowledge it when they debate the issues in public. What the staffs did for Congress in this case, therefore, was cover the fig leaf with the emperor's new clothes.

This conclusion surely is not limited to the natural-gas controversy. Members of Congress generally seem to prefer using the new quantitative rhetoric of social science to discussing the unquantifiable but more informative assumptions on which the numbers rest. If members are ever to get any beneficial use from quantitative analysis, however, they must learn to uncover, compare, and evaluate the unquantifiable assumptions. However, even if a few members have the patience and skill to do this, none has the time. As is true in so many of the ways Congress uses its staff, the members want other people to do work they do not have time to do themselves. But once the work is done, the result is even more work the members do not have time to do. Staff analysis does free Congress from its dependence on the administration's or other outsiders' conclusions, but it fails in its more basic task of informing deliberation. In addition—ironically— it creates a new dependence, that of members on their own staffs.

Is there a way out of this dilemma? I believe there is, in principle, but implementing it would be extremely difficult. In principle, members should direct analysts to provide clear statements of their assumptions at the beginning of their reports. These statements should not be mere lists, or else members will assume—as Senator Jackson and others did in debate—that all assumptions sound equally good, and decide that they are incapable of choosing among them. This attitude, shared widely among elected officials, is flatly wrong. Members of Congress often are in a better position to choose among the assumptions than analysts are. What the members cannot do is tell what quantitative results will flow from a given set of assumptions. Therefore, the most important service an analyst could render would be an elaboration of each assumption underlying a quantitative conclusion, together with a discussion of competing assumptions considered by the analyst and the arguments for (and against) preferring each assumption over its competitors.

Unfortunately, there are two practical impediments to achieving this goal. First, members may hesitate to debate assumptions for political reasons. Second, very few analysts are capable of identifying all their assumptions, let alone articulating them clearly to their political superiors. This weakness, particularly apparent in the way analysts treat their assumptions about what is just or equitable, is a direct result of their education. They are trained, in economics and policy-evaluation courses, to churn out endless tables about the "equity impact" of a given policy choice. By "equity impact," the analysts mean—without a single exception in my experience—the way a given program distributes benefits to the poor, the middle class, and the rich. Certainly this is one important consideration. It may not be the only one, however, as the underlying disagreement between Schlesinger and Stockman should make clear. Whether it should be the dominant one in any given case is something politicians should debate, not let the analysts assume. If one argues that equity or justice may involve more than distribution, however, most analysts shrug off the statement as a "value preference," a prejudice not subject to rational deliberation. All values, ultimately, are fig leaves, and the only thing left for members to debate is the numbers. Never mind that the premise forcing the debate into the realm of numbers leaves the numbers on a foundation of quicksand. The numbers *sound* more solid and, therefore, if not questioned too closely, seem more persuasive.

There is a way out of this, but it may be very difficult to put into effect. Members do make most of their political decisions on political grounds—that is, on the basis of assumptions about distributive justice, commutative justice (rewards based on desert), the nature of international relations, the proper balance between private enterprise and government regulation, and so forth. What they need to do is bring these judgments out into the open and give them the dignity they deserve in debate and deliberation. Only then can cost-benefit analysis be put in a worthwhile perspective.

Restoring political deliberation to a position of dignity will be no small task. First, the elected officials have to be persuaded that it should be done. This might be possible, since most members understand that numbers are inherently their servants, not their masters. Members have to put the numbers in a subordinate place, without going so far as to see them as mere tools for cynical manipulation.

Once this step is accomplished—if it can be—the members have to implement it. They would have to insist that any analyst they hire have an education much broader than that now available from most economics departments or schools of public policy. Members may not be in a position, however, to remedy the tunnel vision that now afflicts the compartmentalized faculties of graduate education in this country. As an alternative, they could expand their staffs to make sure that people with training in the natural sciences and in political philosophy help review and expose the assumptions of cost-benefit studies. The only other approach would be for them to do the work themselves. That, however, would presuppose a drastic reduction in Congress's workload. If the members were prepared to accept doing less, they would not have let their staffs grow so much in the first place.

# 6

# American Statesmanship: Old and New

*Herbert J. Storing*

"Statesmanship" is almost un-American. The word has an elitist and obsolete ring. I will use it, nevertheless, both because it is serviceable enough to refer to the practice (and the theory of the practice) of government rather broadly understood, and because I want to try to rehabilitate, to some extent, an older view. I shall be concerned not so much with the practice of statesmanship as with the way Americans in significant public office, from the president down through at least the upper levels of the bureaucracy, understand their public roles (to use a much more fashionable term).

My beginning point is the observation that there is a strong tendency to resolve the role of the public official into two simple elements: populism, or radical democracy, and scientific management. Since I will be trying to follow some very accessible, though often vaguely understood and expressed, ideas to their roots, I shall not begin with any attempt at precise or elaborate definition—premature definition obscures the interesting questions. I refer to the broad sets of ideas these terms immediately call to mind. They are admittedly vague and they will need refinement and explanation, but they will turn out, as our common language so often does, to identify rather well the kernel of the principles involved. These elements not only tend to characterize American "statesmanship" (and it is precisely because they characterize it that the word "statesmanship" no longer seems to fit), they also are responsible for its characteristic narrowness.

I do not claim that American statesmen always *act* in terms of these principles. Indeed one of the facts of their lives is that they find that they cannot do so. They act in many ways as statesmen have traditionally acted, as leaders trying to deal with problems justly and prudently on their merits. But they have, to a very large extent, lost the understanding of the legitimacy of nonpopulist, non-scientific-management decision making. They "do" statesmanship in the broader and more traditional sense, but they do not understand it. Therefore, they often do not do it very well. While there is much truth in the frequent criticism that our representatives and (especially) our officials are unfeeling and arrogant in their indifference to opinions and concerns other than their own, the more profound phenomenon, I think, is their lack of confidence in their own judgments.

They are rather good at articulating consensus. They are usually reasonably good at implementing clear-cut goals. Much of the time, however, there is no consensus to articulate, or it is foolish or unjust. Most of the time, the goals are not very clear or are in conflict, and their implementation has to be pursued under conditions that do not stand still for the principles of scientific management to be applied. Nonpopulist, nonscientific concerns seem even in American democracy to be at the heart of statesmanship; yet the American statesman is likely to believe that they are not really his proper business, even when he spends most of his time with them. The result is that these nonpopulist, nonscientific sides of American statesmanship tend to be done poorly and, even when done well, tend to be done under cover.

While I shall not here be much concerned specifically with presidential statesmanship, President Carter does provide an instructive case in point. It has become almost a truism that Jimmy Carter, who once seemed such an exotic in presidential politics, is emphatically in the mainstream. His first presidential campaign was built around the two themes that I have suggested are the dominant themes of contemporary American statesmanship: populism and scientific management. The American government was to be brought up to the level of the American people by opening up that government and making it more responsive to the healthy good sense and compassion of the people. ("Make the government as good as the people.") Carter's second theme—the answer to the question of what the candidate would actually *do* when he had opened up the government to the popular impulse—was the promise to reorganize thoroughly the whole government, to reduce the great number of agencies, to cut away at excessive bureaucracy, to improve planning, and to eliminate vast inefficiencies. In short, the promise was to make the government an efficient instrument for doing what the people, now again in control of their own government, want done. Once we became accustomed to the style and the accent, we saw that what was distinctive about the Carter campaign rhetoric was precisely the clarity with which it expressed the distinctive themes of American statesmanship.

There are two qualifications to these observations. First, I have not referred to another strand of the Carter rhetoric, namely, a version of Protestant fundamentalism. In this he is, again, representative of American statesmanship as a whole. In leaving the religious strain of American statesmanship out of account, I admit the incompleteness of my sketch, while also indicating my opinion that this strain would not turn out to be bedrock. A second qualification is closer to my present concern. For better or worse (and opinion on that varies sharply), once in office President Carter did not behave the way his campaign rhetoric indicated that he would behave. True, the populist style was ably, even brilliantly, maintained, and the President pressed hard the theme of technical efficiency, in his reorganization plans, his energy proposals, his decision to drop the development of the B-1 bomber, and so forth. Yet, in substance, President Carter acted very much as other middle-of-the-road presidents have usually acted, attempting to respond to specific policy questions prudently and on their merits, within limits enclosed by popular opinion, but with a willingness to stand against popular opinion and to lead it when that seems wise and possible.

It is arguable that President Carter understood quite well the limits of populism and scientific management and built a rhetoric from them, in quite a clear-headed way, in order, first, to secure office, and then, once in office, to provide the shell for a much broader, more traditional statesmanship. The thrust of this paper is to doubt the feasibility, at least on any significant scale or over any considerable period of time, of a statesmanship in which there is such a sharp difference between style and substance.

At the level of scholarship or "theory," almost all political scientists understand American statesmanship in terms of some combination or variance of the two principles I have identified. Compared to this basic agreement, their disagreements, which seem so compelling in the discipline, are secondary. Scholars in public administration debate the principles of efficient management, the connection between efficiency and "responsibility" (which is understood as responsiveness ultimately to popular will), and the extent to which the science of administration can be divorced in theory and practice from the requirements of democratic responsiveness. Students of American politics debate how adequately the American system collects and orders and gives effect to public opinion. A human relations expert criticizes the formal organization tradition for inadequately perceiving the human requisites of true efficiency. A Richard Neustadt criticizes the President's Committee on Administrative Management for its preoccupation with administrative arrangements and its failure to see the importance of the president's task of persuasion and consensus building. The pluralists criticize the anti-elite theorists for their simplification of democracy and their failure to see the varied and subtle texture of American society. The differences among academic students of American politics are great and the debate is vigorous and often illuminating. Nonetheless, with very rare exceptions (including some parts of the fast-disappearing discipline of constitutional law), the bedrock of principle from which all else derives in American politics is seen to be popular opinion and scientific management. The articulation of these principles and their relation to one another is the whole substance of American politics.

These themes of populism and scientific management are pervasive and deep. They are not, I repeat, always the terms in which American statesmen act; they are not always explicit in specific policy discussions; they are often ignored or overridden in specific decisions. But they are the general terms in which American statesmanship presents and understands itself and is understood both by the people at large and by those whose business it is to study and understand it.

## The Decay of Democratic Statesmanship

That there has been a broad change since the beginnings of the American republic in both the theory and practice of what may loosely be called democratic statesmanship is widely agreed, and the rough outlines of that change are not in much dispute. American political society, and with it American statesmanship, has become much less elitist or, in the older term, aristocratic, and much more democratic or popular. The general view is that that is an improvement, a maturation, a sloughing-off of elements alien to American democracy properly understood. I will try to establish, on the contrary, that from the point of view of the Founders this change represents a decay, and that that point of view makes sense. I will also try to give some account of the main elements of that decay before reflecting on its broad significance.

The indispensable beginning point is to take seriously the Framers' commitment to popular government. This commitment stands out boldly in almost all they said and did; and yet it is seldom seen today for what it was. Part of the reason for this is our tendency to assume that men (and especially "elites") always act for reasons other than those they profess. Even if we overcome that paralyzing and self-defeating premise, we stumble on the Framers' persistent and often sharp criticisms of democracy. They seem to be either hypocritical or half-hearted in their commitment to popular government.

91

The explanation at this level is simple and, it seems to me, altogether compelling. Martin Diamond spent much of his scholarly life trying to show that the Framers' devotion to popular government was the devotion of a true friend, who sees the defects of his friend, studies them, and combats them so that they should not destroy the thing he loves. Popular government is good, but it is problematic. It is not, in this, different from any other kind of government, as Madison explained so well to Jefferson (who understood the point, though he understood it differently from Madison). Each government has an evil tendency that is connected to its own vital principle. In a monarchy it is the king who must be watched; in an oligarchy, the rich; in a popular government, the people. Democracy is a problem in the United States precisely because of the extent to which the people are made the ruler. The beginning point, then, is that popular government is good but problematic in its own way, the specific danger being majority foolishness or tyranny. Democratic statesmanship must be understood, above all, in the light of that great danger, which implies its great task.

At the time of the American founding, the traditional solution to this problem was to build into the government representation of social elements that could check one another, and particularly the *demos*, with the aim of securing the benefits of all and resisting the dangers of each. The American Constitution of 1787 rested on a rejection of this traditional solution. Part of the reason was the unavailability in the United States of the elements of the traditional mixed regime, and especially of a hereditary aristocracy. We do not, the American Founders often said, have the materials for such a mixture. A deeper reason, and the reason most of the Americans thought their solution to the problem was superior even to the admirable and time-tested British regime, was that in the modern mixed regime there was inherent a degree of deception, of resting the working government on appearances rather than on fundamental truths. The traditional mixed regime, as the Americans knew it from Blackstone and Montesquieu, softened the truth of original human equality with the willingness of men to take their places in a natural-seeming hierarchy. It relied heavily on a traditional class of leaders disposed to public service and popularly accepted as entitled to it. The problem was how to secure the benefits of the traditional mixed government without the materials and without the myths and deceptions that such governments involve. The Constitution of 1787 was the Founders' answer.

From the point of view of traditional mixed government, this Constitution looks "democratic"; from the point of view of simple democracy it looks "mixed." Both of these terms were sometimes used by the Founders, but the more common and accurate designations were "popular" and "complex." James Wilson caught the essence, I think, in this characterization:

> In its principles, Sir, it is purely democratical; varying indeed, in its form, in order to admit all the advantages, and to exclude all the disadvantages which are incidental to the known and established constitutions of government. But when we take an extensive and accurate view of the streams of power that appear through this great and comprehensive plan, when we contemplate the variety of their directions, the force and dignity of their currents, when we behold them intersecting, embracing, and surrounding the vast possessions and interests of the continent, and when we see them distributing on all hands beauty, energy and riches, still, however numerous and wide their courses, however diversified and remote the blessings they diffuse, we shall be able to trace them all to one great and noble source, THE PEOPLE.[1]

This government is popular but not simply popular. It does not, however, rely on mystery or myth to check the fundamental popular impulse. "Nondemocratic" "elements" are at work (though not nondemocratic social entities, in Wilson's description), but they are out in the open. This government is like a glass-enclosed clock. Its "works" are visible to all and must be understood and accepted by all in order to function properly. Not many of the Framers were quite as confident as Wilson of the reasonableness of the people, but the government they constructed was nevertheless understood by them all to be unusual in the relatively small demands it placed on a political aristocracy and in the relatively great demands it placed on the people. The Senate was to make its distinctive contribution, for example, not because it consists of people presumed to have some superior title to rule or people with huge social influence derived from family tradition or wealth, but mainly because the interest of the men in the Senate is constitutionally tied to certain "senatorial" duties and because the people would *see*, over a relatively short time, the benefits of such a nonpopular institution.

There were men of the founding generation who found this solution facile and feeble. Alexander Hamilton's reservations are the most pertinent for our present purpose. Hamilton feared that there

---

[1] John Bach McMaster and Frederick D. Stone, eds., *Pennsylvania and the Federal Constitution, 1787–1788* (Lancaster: Historical Society of Pennsylvania, 1888), p. 11.

would be nothing in the new government (and the new society) strong enough to check or channel the reigning popular impulse. Hamilton doubted the effectiveness of the Virginia plan (put forward in the Constitutional Convention by Madison, Randolph, and others) to check the excesses of democracy that had been experienced in many of the states. "A democratic assembly is to be checked by a democratic senate, and both these by a democratic chief magistrate," Hamilton wrote.[2] This looked to him like "pork still, with a little change of the sauce." [3]

While Hamilton labored brilliantly to explain and to defend and to operate this Constitution, his earlier reservations revived, as is well known, as he saw what he thought to be the weakness of the elements in the Constitution designed to check democratic foolishness and injustice. Tocqueville confirms this view, but at the same time presents a wider or at least a different horizon. Even more directly pertinent are the more modest administrative histories of Leonard D. White. It is striking that when White looked at the actual conduct of the government in the early years, including both the Federalist and Jeffersonian periods, it was characterized by what he called "administration by gentlemen." The federal government in its early years was operated by a relatively small group of men, who were socially prominent and who took their bearings from English notions of the right and, more especially, the obligation of members of the class of gentlemen to serve their country by conducting its affairs, and to do that with wisdom, honesty, and public spirit. To the extent that White is correct, it appears the actual conduct of the government then depended crucially on the existence of the political influence of a class of gentlemen, with an ability and a commitment to prudent statesmanship for which the Framers of the Constitution had made no provision. Once the residual, English-based gentry was used up, there was little to preserve or maintain it, and the underlying populism—Hamilton's "pork"—took full command.

I exaggerate, of course. The constitutional scheme of checks and balances continued to function (indeed, in a certain sense, came into its own) under the Jacksonians. If the gentry were swept aside, if demagoguery thrived, the results were still mixed. Jackson's claims for the democratic presidency (accompanied by a certain notion of administration) were challenged, deflected, blunted by men in the Senate and the courts acting much as Madison expected they would

---

[2] Max Farrand, ed., *The Records of the Federal Convention of 1787*, vol. 1, rev. ed. (New Haven: Yale University Press, 1966), p. 310.
[3] Ibid., p. 301.

act. But I am here following one strand of American history and American political thinking. It is not the only strand; it may or may not turn out to be the strongest and most persistent one; but it does seem to be the one most clearly tied to the self-understanding of American statesmen. It became increasingly difficult as the nineteenth and twentieth centuries wore on for American statesmen to see themselves politically as anything more than mouthpieces of popular opinion.

The story we are recounting is completed, in the decisive sense, with civil-service reform, which is the end of democratic statesmanship and the beginning of the contemporary decay of practical statesmanship. The Jacksonian doctrine of rotation (and the Jacksonian program in general) was meant to take the government out of the hands of the few and give it to the many. As rotation declined into spoils, however, it seemed that the result had been to turn over the government from an honest and competent aristocracy to a dishonest and incompetent one. Indeed the concern of the civil-service reform movement that began to build after the Civil War was fundamentally with government dishonesty rather than with government incompetence. Like the Jacksonians, the civil-service reformers' concern was political and moral; and like the Jacksonians the civil-service reformers sought to remove an illegitimate and corrupting obstruction that had grown up in the way of the free, healthy, spontaneous expression of the political will of the American people. The civil-service reform movement is today often described as having been "elitist" and antidemocratic. It involved a "good-government" elite attempting to destroy the vulgar, corrupt, unsystematic, but democratic functioning of patronage-based political parties. This is not inconsistent with the civil-service reformers' view of themselves as returning to the principles of the Founders. But what both this self-understanding and this sociological view of the civil-service reform movement missed is that the reformers had rejected, or forgotten, the central element in the Founders' statesmanship, namely, a sense of the problematic character of democracy. In this fundamental respect they stood with the Jacksonians against the Founders.

Even that, however, is not precise enough. Democracy was in a way still seen as problematic by the reformers, but the locus of the problem had shifted for them from politics to administration. They believed that democracy itself is not unproblematic (the problem here is clearing away the rubble of various kinds that obstructs it), but its implementation *is* unproblematic.

This prepared the way for the next and, as it were, final step in the development of American statesmanship, the science of administration or scientific management. Before turning to that, however, it may be useful to summarize and to reflect on the significance of this development. Leonard D. White described this whole development as a healthy working through of the basic principle of the American republic (again Tocqueville's similar but more critical account is pertinent). As White saw it, bringing into focus a very widespread view, the development ran as follows: first came the Federalist period, characterized by elitist politics plus sound administration; then the Jacksonian period, characterized by democratic politics and unsound administration; and now, a "new Hamiltonianism," characterized by the return, as a result of civil-service reform, to the sound administration of the Founders but now in the service of democratic politics.[4] This view misses three major considerations: (1) The old Hamiltonianism was not antidemocratic, but it was concerned with the problematic character of democracy. (2) Democracy is still problematic; and in losing the sense of that problem (however much the Framers may have missed solving it), the new Hamiltonianism is shallow in the decisive respect. (3) The administrative theory and practice of the old Hamiltonianism, although it was indeed related to scientific management, had a common-sense quality that may have given it more severe limits in some respects than modern administrative science but also a breadth and soundness that today's understanding of administration lacks. To that second aspect of the decay of American statesmanship I now turn.

## The Decay of Rational Statesmanship

When Woodrow Wilson called in 1887 for a new science of administration he saw himself as building upon and to some extent restoring the work of the Founders. With the decisive victory of liberal democratic theory, the making of the U.S. Constitution, and the repair of the major defect of that Constitution in the Civil War, the great task of regime building and constitution making was finished. There would still be a need to extend liberal democracy to other parts of the world and a continuing need to modify and repair its constitutional structure. Nonetheless, the locus of the decisive problems of government had shifted from questions of constitution making and high politics to questions of administration. Wilson sought, then, to turn attention from largely obsolete and fruitless political controversy

---

[4] See Leonard D. White's introduction to Lynton K. Caldwell's *The Administrative Theories of Hamilton and Jefferson*, as quoted in Louis C. Gawthrop, *The Administrative Process and Democratic Theory* (Boston: Houghton Mifflin, 1970), p. 5.

to the pressing and still unsolved problems of running the Constitution. Political theory had had its day; the task for today and tomorrow was the development and application of administrative theory. Wilson proposed that the democracies look to the systematic development of administration that had taken place under more autocratic governments, with the view to developing and learning to use the science of administration, the fundamental premise of which is that there is "but one rule of good administration for all governments alike." [5]

In many important ways, Wilson's proposal and the project of administrative science and practice that followed from it were indeed extensions of the Founders' own project. In the most crucial sense, it can be said that, for the Founders, the problem of government is a matter of administration. Government was no longer seen as a grappling with various and conflicting claims to rule, claims to determine the ends and character of social life. Instead, they believed the legitimate end of government is fixed: the securing of individual rights. In question, in terms of both forms of government and their operation, are the arrangements and policies that under given circumstances would be the best means to that fixed end.

This is the reason that discussions by the founding generation of forms of government have the curiously shallow quality that has frustrated so many analysts. Monarchy no longer "rides tilt against democracy," as Woodrow Wilson put it.[6] There were still differences, and forms of government were still important (see *Federalist*, No. 70), but they no longer carried anything like their traditional freight. Government was no longer seen as directing and shaping human existence, but as having the much narrower (though indispensable) function of facilitating the peaceful enjoyment of the private life. In this view, government and the whole public sphere are decisively instrumental; government is reduced to administration. Questions of forms of government, too, become instrumental. Much less is *at stake* in a dispute between "democracy" and "monarchy," for example. The question is merely what kind of governmental arrangements will, under given conditions, be most likely to secure the aggregate of individual liberty, which it is the business of any government to secure. (This is why constitutional and administrative questions, in contrast to *political* questions, are closely related for Wilson.)

---

[5] Woodrow Wilson, "The Study of Administration," *Political Science Quarterly* (June 1887). An abridged version can be found in Gawthrop, *Administrative Process and Democratic Theory*, p. 20.
[6] Gawthrop, *Administrative Process and Democratic Theory*, pp. 77–78.

"Statesmanship" in such a government is diminished in proportion. It can reasonably be called administration, though it may be administration of a rather high and demanding kind. The moral demands on statesmen in such a government are reduced to a commitment to serve the "permanent and aggregate interests of the society," as Madison called them. The intellectual demands are reduced to the formulation and implementation of appropriate means to fairly limited ends. To the American Founders, however, even these demands seemed too great. The moral demands on the statesman were further reduced by putting him in a constitutional position, so far as possible, where his private interests would coincide with his public duty. The whole complex system of checks and balances and related constitutional devices have this aim. The intellectual demands (our special concern here) would be reduced through the development of the sciences dealing with the main areas of the statesman's (now rather limited) concerns. Thus, to the Founders, the science of economics—or rather political economy—is queen; derivative from this are the subordinate sciences of, for example, military administration, governmental budgeting and accounting, and the arrangement of public offices. The American statesman of the future would be not a George Washington but a Robert Morris, a man whose private interests were closely tied to his country's fortunes and whose statesmanship consisted of the knowledge that a merchant and financier has of the way society works.

In sum, then, the American Founders' view of statesmanship could be described as follows. There is never needed that kind of statesmanship which had formerly been regarded as its essence: great, "way of life"-setting, character-forming political leadership. That kind of leadership was based upon a misapprehension of political life, a failure to understand its decisively instrumental function. There may be needed, however, rarely but occasionally, what might be called high American statesmanship, or high liberal statesmanship, comparable to that of the Founders themselves. The requirements here are an extraordinary (and perhaps ultimately inexplicable) devotion to public duty and an understanding of the principles of governmental structure and operation of the broadest and deepest kind. Note that this statesmanship is still, in a fundamental sense, "administrative"; it ministers to the private sphere essentially by securing private rights. Most of the time, however, an even narrower statesmanship will be sufficient: the activities of reasonably decent and well-informed men, guided by the constitutional system and by moral and prudential maxims derived from widely understood principles of political economy, military science, public finance, and so forth.

Just as the popular principle became radicalized, so did the "science" of government or administration become radicalized. The Founders' maxims of administrative statesmanship became Woodrow Wilson's "one rule of good administration for all governments alike," which in turn became Frederick Taylor's "one best method," and that in turn became the "maximizing" model (and all of its various elaborations and qualifications) of contemporary decision-making science.

Frederick Taylor is perhaps the crucial turning point. Taylor insisted that his techniques—such as time-and-motion studies—must never be separated from the broader "philosophy of scientific management." That philosophy was a simplification of modern liberalism. Taylor saw scientific management as the working principle of a whole social system in which there is ultimately social harmony among apparently competing groups and individuals. He believed that once the true principles of organized activity are discovered and applied through scientific management, political and social conflict, which is based upon ignorance and misunderstanding, will be dispelled. Compared to the Founders' view of American statesmen, Taylor's administrative statesman is relatively narrow.

The context of the older statesmanship was still a political or constitutional order which was, indeed, expected to limit the statesman's horizon; but that horizon was, nevertheless, a political one, and that was reflected in his everyday judgments. For Taylor, on the other hand, the context is a presumed natural harmony. There is ultimately no need for politics—either as providing a broad political order within which economic activity is pursued or (therefore) as adjusting competing and (in terms of mere self-interest) irreconcilable demands. Taylor did not in fact entirely escape the need for the more traditional moral and political judgment. The increase in pay for Schmitt, the carrier of iron hogs, was not to be in proportion to his greater efficiency (which resulted merely from his willingness to accept the commands of the scientifically informed supervisor); it was to be enough to stimulate him to raise the level of his private life, but not so much as to demoralize him. It is not clear where the standard for such judgments comes from in Taylor's scheme (though it should be noted that it is not clear either where the standard for equivalent decisions by traditional liberal statesmen comes from). Nor is it clear why the scientific manager does not attempt to pay Schmitt as little as possible in order to keep an unfair share of the benefits of increased efficiency for himself. The whole problem of the fidelity of the statesman, with which the Framers were so deeply and, on the whole, effectively concerned, was largely ignored by Taylor. Not surprisingly, Taylorism came to be, or at least was widely thought to be, an instrument of management. It became, after all, part of a broader political context, for which Taylorism itself could not account and to which it could not direct itself.

This "philosophy" of scientific management, which seemed to Taylor so fundamental, quickly dropped away, distorting Taylorism in ways that seemed to have been invited by Taylor (as Taylorism distorted the administrative thought of the Founders). What was left was the pool of techniques of scientific management, the best known of which are time-and-motion studies, and the notion of the "one best method."

> Now, among the various methods and implements used in each element of each trade there is always one method and one implement which is quicker and better than any of the rest. And this one best method and best implement can only be discovered or developed through a scientific study and analysis of all of the methods and implements in use, together with accurate, minute, motion and time study. This involves the gradual substitution of science for rule of thumb throughout the mechanic arts.[7]

This notion, which is basic to scientific management and all its heirs, would have seemed strange to the Founders with their more common-sense notions of administrative science. Yet, it could be argued that Taylor was merely making clear and explicit what the earlier science implied: that the theoretical challenge is to develop that science of "management" in the broadest sense that will ultimately or in principle utterly displace the ad hoc, muddled, and inefficient lore of the traditional craftsman, as well as the ad hoc, muddled, and inefficient judgment of the traditional statesman.

What I have called scientific management in the broadest sense has taken a further large step beyond Taylorism, but in the same direction. Taylor can be understood as radicalizing the Founders' attempt to free the statesman from major concern with the broadest ends of his activities. The statesman provided for by the Founders "works" the system without having to try to follow his decisions to their broadest ends; the Taylor manager similarly develops his science secure in the knowledge that better means will naturally lead to good ends. In these ways both the Founders' statesman and Taylor's statesman are substantially relieved of responsibility for considering the highest or broadest ends. In the concrete situation, however, both are emphatically end-oriented. Taylorism is a science or means to

---

[7] Frederick Winslow Taylor, *The Principles of Scientific Management* (New York: Harper and Brothers, 1911), p. 25.

given ends. The science was instrumental in the way administration had always been understood to be instrumental, as subordinate to given ends. The rationale of practical statesmanship became severely narrowed, but it was not transformed.

This traditional way of thinking about administration has the great advantage that the given ends guide and limit the search for means. That advantage, however, is purchased at a price that is scientifically unacceptable. The standard scientific formula becomes: Given a comprehensive measurable statement of ends, there is but one best means. It became increasingly clear that such a requirement is not only impossible in practice (that is not regarded as fatal), but also inadequate in principle. "Ends" are misleading reflections of prescientific judgmental statesmanship. What common sense calls "ends" are ultimately mere wants, and one cannot be expected to know what one wants until one knows what one might have and at what cost. The very language of means-ends is not merely imprecise or approximate, it is essentially misleading. The decisive break comes with its replacement by something like a "behavior-alternative" model (what are my possible courses of action and which do I want?) or a utility-maximization model freed from the teleological implications of the means-ends, but now at the price of crushing informational and calculational demands and utter subjection to essentially arbitrary preference.

This independence from ends, and its accompanying benefits and problems, is what characterized the most recent version of scientific management. While it is surely true, as earlier laborers in the vineyard of scientific management complained, that such fashionable schemes as "systems analysis" and Program Planning and Budgeting System (PPBS) are in many ways less new and original than they claim, there is today a rather widespread understanding of the fact that what scientific management has been moving toward is not statesmanship, and not even administration or management, but rather economizing in the true sense.

The contribution of "systems analysis" is to clarify and elaborate the proposition that all practical rationality, the rationality of administration, the rationality of choice, is economic rationality. "It should go without saying that all decision-making persons or groups attempt to economize, in the true sense of the word. That is, they try to make the 'most,' as they conceive of the 'most,' of whatever resources they have." [8]

---

[8] Richard N. McKean, "The Role of Analytical Aids," in Gawthrop, *Administrative Process and Democratic Theory*, p. 253.

With this understanding clearly in mind, the new science of choice can overcome the two great defects of traditional statesmanship, which even the earlier forms of scientific management had not altogether corrected: its preoccupation with ends and its inability or unwillingness to replace mere maxims of action with objective measurement. In his preoccupation with given ends—those that seem important at the moment or those he is administratively responsible for—the traditional statesman or even the fairly sophisticated "manager" has failed to see the essentially economic character of all decision making. Thus, one of the men who helped to apply the new understanding to the Department of Defense, where it has had its greatest (though still disputed) success, explained that in 1961 military planning was in "disarray" because of the separation of military planning and fiscal planning. Military plans were made more or less incrementally and in terms of certain presumed military needs and objectives, with the price tag tacked on afterwards. With the help of PPBS, the economic character of the decisions was recognized; thus costs and national security objectives were linked at the outset, while systems analysis provided quantitative information on various possibilities.

Although it is not always easy to understand just how far the claims of systems analysis extend, in general it can be said that greater sophistication about the economic underpinnings and techniques of quantification has been accompanied by greater sophistication in claims about practical applicability. The proponents of systems analysis are, generally, considerably less expansive than Taylor, for example, in the extent of their claims to replace traditional common-sense judgment. They emphasize that quantitative analysis can clarify and make more intelligent, but cannot displace, the nonscientific decision of the responsible administrator. Both implicitly (for example, in the "end" implications of "program" budgeting) and explicitly (for example, in various models of what Herbert Simon called "satisficing"), the proposals of systems analysis concede and even grapple with the limits of their science. If the practical claim is muted, the theoretical claim is even sharper and more comprehensive. Systems analysis admits, indeed emphasizes, that it can never absorb completely the "practical" side of practical reason. At the same time, it clearly affirms that it does in principle comprehend the "rational" side of practical reason. Systems analysis (or the science of the economics of decision making) is not all that there is to practical reason in decision making, but it is all there is to the *reason* of practical reason.

## Some Common-Sense Corrections

Does this more or less historical analysis help us to understand contemporary issues of American statesmanship? It seems to me that it does. It encourages us to revive for consideration some rather obvious, useful common-sense observations about American statesmanship, what it is and what it ought to be. It also leads into some less obvious, more fundamental theoretical issues, the practical thrust of which is much more obscure, but which are probably determinative in the long run.

**Populism.** It is not difficult to grasp and to be persuaded by the need a democracy has of regulation and guidance in the face of some of its own tendencies toward foolishness and injustice. If we can add to our rather sharp consciousness of the dangers of "elites" a recollection of the dangers of majorities, our statesmanship will be better grounded. Indeed this lesson has never been forgotten in practice. What has been neglected is its understanding and justification in principle. Government still acts in opposition to simple democracy (when it secures the rights of minorities and individuals, for example), but mostly we talk as if the solution to the problems of democracy is more democracy. That is why there is a persistent *tendency* to resolve more or less complex notions of American democracy into some kind of simple populism.

This simplistic talk at the level of principle tends to undermine more prudent views at the level of practice. Even the modern Supreme Court, the strongest bastion of nonpopulist principle, has an increasingly difficult time giving an account of itself. Nevertheless, in the courts there is still a self-conscious and principled capacity to resist mere majoritarianism, weakened as this may have become. In the other parts of the government, such a capacity is much less evident. One of the results is, I think, an undermining of the statesman's confidence in his own judgment, in the legitimacy of relying on his own judgment even in the face of popular disagreement. The further and even more harmful result is that the people at large are constantly taught by their statesmen's rhetoric that their opinion is the touchstone of politics. Because this is not the case in practice, and cannot be the case in any respectable regime, the contradiction strains the system, driving true leadership underground and depriving the system of popular confidence. The whole doctrine of elitism, in both its popular and scholarly forms, owes much to the absence in our public rhetoric (and behind that in our scholarly understanding) of a justification of the role of an "elite," a not simply responsive statesmanship in American democracy.

The danger of populism to popular government has to be met, I think, at two levels. At the level of institutions, the problem is basically recovering (perhaps in different forms) the lessons of the Framers. I have mentioned the Supreme Court, and it is surely vital to our whole constitutional system that the broad understanding and acceptance of the legitimacy of such a contrademocratic institution, as Alexander Bickel called it, not be lost; or if it has in principle been lost, that it be recovered.

Another institution that has seemed promising to me in this regard is the bureaucracy which, for all its limitations, does introduce into the political system elements of stability, intelligence, and equity that are not altogether dissimilar to the qualities intended to be provided by the original Senate. The advantage of the bureaucracy from this point of view is its very invincibility (a democracy has a much harder time dispensing with the bureaucracy than with the Senate, as Weber—with somewhat different intentions—has shown). The disadvantage is the bureaucracy's narrowness and its strong tendency towards the merely technical, a tendency strengthened under modern doctrines of scientific management. A properly schooled bureaucracy might, however, be a solidly based source of the intelligence, stability, equity, and public-spiritedness that a democracy needs.

But institutional arrangements are probably not sufficient, and the degree to which the Founders relied on them may partly explain the power of the populist principle. For the institutions require what I have argued has been seriously lacking, namely public justification and, therefore, continued legitimacy in the eyes of the people, who are the ultimate rulers. What some of the Founders neglected is that in a popular government, however much it is modified with various "sauces" (and the bureaucracy is a fairly penetrating one), the people have to be reasoned with by their statesmen. This means reasoning not only at the level of specific policies but also at the level of constitutional principle. Precisely because the American government is so transparent, relatively speaking, so little reliant on lords, kings, and priests, American statesmen must keep alive its basic rationale. At the least this means not playing the easy game of populist rhetoric, which cannot but undermine, in the long run, the capacity of the system to act well. At the most it means finding ways of reinforcing and deepening the people's common-sense understanding that government, even popular government, is more than a matter of registering and implementing dominant opinion.

This task of leadership is crucial, and it provides a kind of rough test of contemporary statesmen. Any American statesman whose public face is populistic is not performing his highest duty, no matter how prudent and successful his specific policies may be. This points us, however, to the deeper consideration to which I have made reference. The founding generation, people and leaders alike, could grasp the principles of checks on popular opinion and could make informed judgments about specific institutions and policies because they were persuaded of the truth of the foundation and end of that government. That there can be majority tyranny is a notion that makes sense to men who see government as designed to secure inalienable rights. If this truth is denied or lost sight of—as is surely the case today—it becomes exceedingly difficult to hold any ground against the populist impulse.

The loose relativism that today penetrates popular political and ethical understanding tends, of course, to support the kind of loose populism I have been examining and criticizing. Such relativism is the ultimate obstacle to any thorough-going mitigation (by which I do not mean some kind of aristocratic displacement) of simplistic democracy. The great popular—and final—challenge today is, "Who's to say?" The question implies not only that it is extremely difficult and dangerous to give anyone (or any governmental institution) the power to "say" what is right or what is to be done, but that there is in principle no way to "say" what is right or what should be done. Liberal government exists in a tension between popular control and individual rights. With the washing away of the ground of individual rights, consent in one form or another seems to be the only place for a statesman to stand.

If this describes the popular view, the scholarly view is fundamentally identical. Almost the whole range of dispute among scholars about how American democracy does and should work takes place within the "consent" arena. What is popular consent? How is it articulated, and how is it to be most accurately recorded and responded to by government? These are the agreed issues. There are occasional forays outside the field of populism, but their general feebleness tends to support my broad point. The "new public administration," for example, has been dissatisfied, mainly on political grounds, with the subordination of the old public administration to dominant public opinion. The *ground* on which the new public administration might resist popular opinion is a treacherous bog consisting of supposed silent or suppressed majorities (a path out of the bog and onto the safe ground of populism again), or an almost undefended commitment to socially disadvantaged people (as the definition of social equality and social consciousness), or a more or less simple existentialism, which the new public administration is not the first to see is the main alternative to democratism. If sheer preference or commitment is all there is, why not mine?

**Scientific Management.** Just as a serious examination of the insufficiency of populism yields a number of common-sense corrections, so does the serious examination of the insufficiencies of scientific management. But as contemporary populism points to the underlying issue of natural rights, so contemporary scientific management points to the underlying issue of the nature of human reason. In this case it may be more helpful to touch (with some apprehension) on this underlying issue before turning to some common-sense thoughts about statesmanship or practical reason. We are not going to be much helped here by the thought of the American Founders. They were far less articulate and self-conscious in their thinking about practical reason, or decision making, or the science of government, than they were about the political side of government. Their thrust was in the direction of systematic science, but this science did not seem to be inconsistent with, or likely to replace, traditional prudence. We who live with the sometimes unintended results of their work and thought need to try to recover and reflect upon some of their more or less hidden assumptions.

Our problem is to understand practical reason or, in the contemporary term, "rational" decision making. The issue is well framed in Herbert Simon's forceful and influential attack on the maxims of so-called practical judgment. Simon's argument is that these maxims, which are supposed to guide practical reason and which are the glory of the "practical man," are in fact empty because they are self-contradictory. For every maxim there is a counter-maxim: look before you leap; he who hesitates is lost. The sum of practical rationality here is zero. If the practical man decides well (for example, if he maximizes his values), either he is lucky or he is proceeding according to a rationality more systematic and scientific than he knows, which it is the business of the science of decision making to elaborate and extend. (This is a theoretical elaboration of Frederick Taylor's scientific management.)

The issue here is, What *is* rational decision making? I think many of the critics of scientific management have given up the game too easily, granting a Simonian understanding of what rational decision making is but contending that the sphere of rationality in decision making is much more limited than Simon and others suggest. Practical judgment turns out to be either an accommodation to practical political necessities or an unavoidable arbitrariness. (It is the current willingness of systems-analysis proponents to admit these limitations on practical rationality that has typically muddled the issue in the current literature.) I think the attack must be carried further.

I will not claim victory here, but I do want at least to open the question whether scientific management misunderstands the essence, if not the scope, of practical rationality. I will frame the issue as a proposition: the two critical principles of the current understanding of practical reason, or rational decision making—the notion of the "one best method" and the assumption that all practical reasoning is essentially economic reasoning—do not make good sense.

As already suggested, the crux of scientific management is the notion of "one best method." Does it not make more sense to say that practically there often *is* no one best method? The road to the one best method is not the road to rationality but to insanity. There are many cases where it just does not matter much which one of alternative choices is made (whether, for example, to ride elevator A or elevator B). It is not rational to worry or calculate much about something that does not matter much, even if one could conceive of and even perhaps discover some marginal benefit one way or the other (elevator A is closer to the entrance and thus more used and thus more worn—or is it therefore better maintained?). In other cases, the difference between alternative possible choices may matter very much, but there may be practically no way to know which one is better. It is likely that the outcomes cannot be known in crucial respects. There is, of course, a good deal of thinking and research on decision making under conditions of uncertainty, but again the premise of this thinking is that these conditions *limit* rationality. My suggestion is the common-sensical and, I think, practically indispensable notion that one of the most important elements of practical reason— or "rational" decision making—is precisely how well or poorly such limits are grappled with.

The man who insists on calculating, and constantly postpones decisions in order to get more information and make more predictions and calculations, is acting *irrationally* in any sensible view, though he is merely persisting in a rational pursuit according to the strict economizing model. Herbert Simon speaks of "bounded rationality," yet he more or less admits that it is only because of these irrational boundaries that any given exercise of rationality makes any sense at all.[9] Simon's main response to the insanity of the maximizing model

---

[9] Herbert Simon, *Administrative Behavior: A Study of Decision Making Processes in Administrative Organization*, 2nd ed. (New York: Macmillan, 1957).

is what he calls "satisficing," which is a much more common-sense (and, incidentally, traditional means-end) approach in which the decision maker is satisfied with the decision that is "good enough" instead of insisting on maximizing. That seems altogether, may we say, reasonable. But for Simon it is a necessary falling short of reason. We "satisfice" because we have not the wits to maximize. If we can maximize, we would be silly to "satisfice." On the contrary, I think we "satisfice" because we have the wits to know that we *cannot* maximize and that we would be insane to try to do so. The notion of the "one best method," that human rationality is the maximization of utility, is, as I have tried to show in an extended analysis of Herbert Simon, a fragile bridge suspended between two great fires, the arbitrariness of preference and the insanity of infinite calculation, by which it is consumed.[10]

The second side of the contemporary view of practical reason is the contention that all practical reasoning, all rational decision making, is essentially economic. That does not mean that there is any claim that all people do act as economizers—or even that anyone actually does it (it turns out to be quite impossible); but so far as they are rational they are economizers. The genius of "economic" rationality is that it is unqualifiably comprehensive and it is also a purely instrumental science. All "ends," "values," are reduced to "utility," which provides the ultimate test of the science of rational choice without threatening its purely instrumental character. Clearly, there is some truth in this whole understanding. To take the previously given example of military planning, it is surely correct that for military planners utterly to ignore questions of cost does involve their avoiding the "hard management choices" that must be made. In government, at least, every decision (well, almost every decision) can be and at some point must be reduced to a decision about budget, about economizing. Clearly, economizing is involved in practical reasoning, is necessary to it; the question is whether that is all there is to it or whether that is truly its essence.

Consider the experience and the character of the Bureau of the Budget or, in its present form, the Office of Management and Budget. The centrality and independence of the OMB are undeniable. It is hard to imagine a government without such an institution performing such a function (though it is perhaps not quite as hard to imagine as we might today think, and the effort might be instructive). It is easy, moreover, to agree that the director of the OMB, whoever he may

---

[10] Herbert Storing, ed., *Essays on the Scientific Study of Politics* (New York: Holt, Rinehart and Winston, 1962), pp. 63–150.

be, is the superior, despite his lack of cabinet position and his lower salary, of most heads of departments. But is it imaginable that the OMB should govern—would that be reasonable? My point is simple, but I think very pertinent to the present issue. It is surely important that generals be compelled to face the issue of cost/benefit, and the people who do that compelling are as vital in practice as that element of practical rationality is vital in principle. But must not generals remain generals? Could the OMB defend the country? Could it conduct foreign relations? Could it protect individual rights?

What we need to consider here is the effect of economic *thinking* and whether its claim to be practical rationality makes sense. Is not the beginning of military rationality some kind of understanding of an adequate defense, rather than some abstract notion of maximizing utility or even the rather less abstract notion of "more bang for the buck"? Are not similar understandings the essential basis for practical rationality in other spheres? The legitimate rights of minorities ought to be secured. Old people ought to be able to live decently. All of these raise or point to economic questions, but they are not "economizing" in themselves. The question is whether such end-oriented views are not independent, indispensable bases of practical rationality.

The crux in practice is what kind of decision results from one view or the other. Grant that a general will make bad decisions if he utterly ignores questions of cost (which the fact of limited resources makes it extremely difficult to do). But then consider what kind of decision the economist is likely to make. Is he not likely to be easily shifted from a "utility" that is costly to one that is less so? Is he not likely to prefer utilities and costs that are measurable over those that are not? I do not claim that the economists *necessarily* make such errors in practical reasoning—any more than it can be claimed that the general is necessarily irresponsible or indifferent to cost/benefit—but that is the tendency.

One of the common criticisms of scientific management in various forms, including systems analysis, is its indifference to structure and institutions and, at the same time, its thoughtless tendency to foster centralized institutions. The basis of this criticism is the traditional fear that the centralization fostered by the pursuit of administrative efficiency will threaten democracy. It should be noted that the claim that scientific management has a centralizing tendency is controversial. Some defenders of systems analysis have contended that it is neutral with regard to structure and indeed can foster decentralization. Taking advantage of an ambiguity that is unresolved in Max Weber's account of bureaucracy, they contend that the development of objectively rational bases of decision reduces the dependence on their authority and therefore on hierarchy. In Weberian terms, the stronger and more comprehensive the definition of jurisdiction, the weaker can be the lines of hierarchical authority (subject, of course, to the necessity of enforcing jurisdictional definitions which are relatively unexplored by scientific management). In practice, surely, and, as I have tried at least to suggest, in principle also, scientific management is centralizing. It is centralizing in the sense that Frederick Taylor understood perfectly well, that the crucial and governing activity is development of the science itself, which can only occur (except derivatively) at the top. It is centralizing, further, to the extent that gaps in the science make it necessary to resort to central *authority* to support the science itself. And it is centralizing to the extent that (presuming a comprehensive science) there remains a continuing need to *enforce* the rational design of the science.

Scientific management radicalizes the claim for "unity" in administration. When Andrew Jackson defended his removal of subordinates even contrary to congressional legislation, he presented a view of administration as well as a view of democracy. Administration was seen as residing crucially in the president with the administration serving as his eyes and hands. The Whig view, on the other hand, rested not only on a different (more "pluralistic") view of American politics but also on a different view of administration. The Whigs saw public administration not as a closed hierarchy leading to the top but as pools of official discretion, loosely connected but largely independent. Jackson and the Whigs were primarily concerned with what today we would call the issue of responsibility—Jackson, to the president; the Whigs, to the law. But the implicit views of public administration are especially interesting here, and the Whig view in particular since it is the one that seems always to lose. This view emphasizes the importance of the exercise of experienced, informed, responsible discretion as the heart of administration. Sound discretion, not obedience to higher command, is the essence of good administration, though both, of course, are always involved. Administrative structures should be built to provide the right conditions for this informed good judgment—independent regulatory commissions are a case in point. The Whig view of administration is modeled, one might say, on the judge. (One could describe modern administrative science as the decisive displacement of the judge as the model administrator by the administrative assistant—even, increasingly, in the courts themselves.) A major aspect of the Whig model was the notion of the judge's responsibility, but I want to point to another side, the kind of practical reason the judge exercises. His judgment here is confined and guided by more or less severe limits of the law, but within these limits the judge is expected to secure a personal grasp on the whole and to exercise his best judgment. He is thus, characteristically, assisted by law clerks, whose very immaturity, transience, and small numbers reinforce the judge's personal responsibility and judgment.

It seems reasonably clear that any government, to be well administered, needs a judicious combination of these two principles—each may appropriately predominate in its own time and place. But what we need to recover is an understanding of the claim of what can be called the judicial model of *rationality*. Partly because of our failure to grasp the *reason* of that model, it always tends to lose out in a contest with centralized, hierarchical rationality.

Perhaps the most striking omission in scientific management is any concern with the moral side of decision making, especially of political decision making. There is some current renewed interest in the ethics of administration or decision making, but it tends to result either in (fringe) codes-of-ethics thinking, the assumption of which is that ethics surround practical decision making but do not really enter into it; or in (sterile) case studies of the confrontation of (arbitrary) public policies and (arbitrary) personal preferences.

What we can roughly but usefully call the moral side of public decision making was for the American Founders the major concern; today the intellectual side has occupied almost the whole ground. Yet in any kind of practical situation the question of the fidelity of the decision maker is crucial. The question that Frederick Taylor could not answer (or could answer only by assuming a simplistic harmony)—why will the scientific manager not try to exploit his workers?—was for the Founders the vital issue of statesmanship.

Robert Hutchins once observed of university administration that the intellectual problems, adapting means to ends, are small compared to the moral problems. A fairly simple example: It is on the whole easier to know that someone does not deserve academic tenure than it is to decide not to give it to him. As I cast my mind back on the many administrative situations I have been involved in, I am struck by the importance of the moral character of the people in charge. I think of a small army unit that constantly threatened to come unhinged under the leadership of an intelligent and able but weak commander and which was held together only by the stern, mule-skinner army morality of an old, extremely inefficient master sergeant. I think of political science departments whose fortunes (so far as they are not determined from the outside) seem to wax and wane far more in rhythm with the integrity and moral stature of department heads than with their administrative ability in the usual sense. I do not mean to assert the simple-minded proposition that good men make good administrators, or even that good administrators need to be good men—although that is not a bad place to start. I think that one could defend the proposition that moral stature is vital to administration or statesmanship of any consequence. And that is precisely what is lacking in our statesmen trained in and oriented to scientific management. They are no more really bad men than really good ones; rather, they tend to be morally uninteresting children. That dimension—moral stature—is missing or severely truncated.

The reference to Robert Hutchins suggests another common-sense correction of the scientific-management view of statesmanship, namely that the good statesman has a good understanding of and commitment to the ends of his organization, whatever they are. University presidents these days tend to be bookkeepers and brokers among their various "constituencies." That may, often, be good enough, but such administrators work in the shadow of men who knew what universities are for and how any particular university fit into that broad function. Greatness in a president of the United States, in a president of a university, in a general of the Army, or in a chief of a governmental bureau is determined among other things by the grasp he has of the *ends* of his organization. A fairly loose grasp may be sufficient most of the time, but even mundane statesmanship is rooted in some such understanding. If an ordinary public servant does not need the grasp of the American regime of a Lincoln, he does need, as John Rohr suggests, at least the grasp of a reasonably competent student of some parts of American constitutional law.[11]

A final common-sense observation, harder to explain and defend, and for that reason more directly pertinent to the underlying question of practical reason, is that the essence of statesmanship is to be found in the old distinction between line and staff. The curious thing about decision-making theory is that it is not about decisions but about getting ready to make decisions. The rationality of scientific management is the rationality of the staff, but it does not reach, it does not treat whatever it is that is finally *decisive*. Decisiveness is, after all, universally acknowledged to be central to good administration of any consequence, yet it has no place in decision-making theory.

---

[11] John A. Rohr, *Ethics for Bureaucrats* (New York: Marcel Dekker, 1978).

EDITORIAL NOTE
*Herbert Storing had not quite completed his work on this essay when he died, suddenly, on September 9, 1977. A comparison of this draft with his outline for the essay indicates that a final section, "Conclusion," was never written. The portion of the outline covering the "Conclusion" is presented below.*

*The reader is cautioned that Mr. Storing may have intended some changes as he developed the ideas from the outline into their final essay form; however, a careful comparison of the outline and the essay as a whole indicates that he followed the outline, as far as he went, quite closely.*

## Conclusion

Authentic American statesmanship has decayed, but it decayed (as it were) from within.
1. Premise: statesmanship is in the service of the private sphere. This means that the activity of statesmanship is not seen as "fulfilling" and tends to be held in low esteem.
2. This is magnified by the American Founders' effort to rely even on this instrumental statesmanship as little as possible.
3. Radicalization of popular principle
4. Radicalization of science as government principle

Thus statesmanship is not much respected; doesn't much respect itself ("civil servants" want to be "professionals" or even "government employees" rather than "civil servants")

Statesmanship tends to narrow itself to the role of the respectable technician, leaving the big decisions to "politicians" who in turn have to find their justification in being spokesmen of the popular will.

There is an alternative tradition, growing out of what the Framers did rather than what they said.

They were pulled between the private and public lives; usually they chose the public, and not merely out of duty (and anyway, what's the basis of that?)

There is also a strain of popular recognition of need for nontechnical leadership and of leaders who see that need and try to meet it; always a presumption against that—which has been radicalized.

(this will not, however, be the last point made)

# 7

# Reflections on Statesmanship and Bureaucracy

*Werner J. Dannhauser*

Custom prescribes the proper approach to the question of "statesmanship and bureaucracy." One is expected to be concerned about the bureaucratic threat to statesmanship. One is supposed to assume that the demand for statesmanship exceeds the supply while the supply of bureaucracy exceeds the demand, and that we would have more statesmanship if we had less bureaucracy. Bureaucracy is to be understood as a kind of fungus, a threat to what has come to be called the machinery of government. The customary view holds statesmanship to be very good and bureaucracy to be very bad; if one were inclined to differ one would speak not of "statesmanship and bureaucracy" but of "politics and the civil service."

The purpose of this paper is to test the customary view by posing a number of questions. What is statesmanship? What is bureaucracy? Is their relationship necessarily an adversary one? How much control do we really have over the presence and absence of statesmanship; of bureaucracy? Is bureaucracy really, as is so often asserted, a left-wing and anticapitalist phenomenon? Is it essentially antidemocratic? Might it be that statesmanship is fully as much a problem for democracy as bureaucracy?

To test the customary view is not necessarily to refute it, but to attempt to understand it better. Though in my opinion many present-day warnings about the dire threat of bureaucracy are exaggerated, to prove even that much requires attention to what the customary views are. Let us, then, begin—and perhaps end—with a decent respect for conventional wisdom, remembering that it is likely to partake not only of the conventional but the wise.

The author is grateful to Peter Katzenstein and Joseph Cropsey.

## The Statesman as a Model of Excellence

Our inquiry deals with statesmanship and statesmen, not politics and politicians. A common man with common sense experiences no particular difficulty in distinguishing between the two sets of terms; neither do statesmen or politicians themselves. Only cynics are likely to dispute the distinction.

Of course, one finds cynics in many professions, including politics. Joe Cannon, speaker of the House of Representatives, was speaking as a cynical politician when he said, early this century, that a statesman is a politician who has been dead a long time,[1] but his statement recognizes the distinction in question. It concedes that while all statesmen are politicians, not all politicians are statesmen. It is cynical in its deliberate refusal to see the whole truth of the matter, for Speaker Cannon surely knew that President Buchanan was a politician who had been dead a long time without ever being or becoming a statesman, while President Washington was still alive when he was first in the hearts of his countrymen, largely for being that very special kind of statesman we call a Founding Father. A statesman is, then, not simply a politician, but an extraordinary politician who exercises wise leadership. It follows that it is a good thing to be a statesman; in fact, it may be the very best thing.

What *is* the best thing for a man to be? Even if we concede that the question may be almost impossible to settle conclusively, the number of reasonable answers to it is by no means large. We are unable to take seriously a man who says that nothing could be finer than to be a barber, or a butcher, or a bureaucrat. On the other hand, we do consider seriously those who say that the best thing to be is a statesman, or a poet, or a philosopher. The prize usually goes to the philosophers, but that may well be because they are the ones who do the ranking, while statesmen are too busy securing for them the conditions of tranquility required for philosophizing. One might add that some very great poets have conceded a kind of superiority to statesmen, as Yeats did when he wrote in 1915:

> I think it better that at times like these
> We poets keep our mouths shut; for in truth
> We have no gift to set a statesman right.[2]

---

[1] Quoted in Morton J. Frisch and Richard G. Stevens, ed. *American Political Thought: The Philosophic Dimension of American Statesmanship* (New York: Scribners, 1971), p. 3. This volume provides a useful background for the topic of this paper.

[2] Quoted in John R. Harrison, *The Reactionaries* (New York: Schocken, 1967), p. 43, in a chapter that illuminates Yeats's politics rather than his poetry, or the intricate and often inscrutable relationship between them.

In any event, a statesman is a model of excellence. We are bemused when a boy tells us he wants to grow up to be a jet pilot and pleased when he informs us he wants to be president. It goes without saying, we think, that he aspires to become a Lincoln rather than a Buchanan. A statesman is not only a model of excellence, but also something many people actually want to become. (A saint is also a model of excellence, but fewer people wish to become saintly.) The presidency of the United States is forever being described as a lonely, killing, thankless job, and the United States is declared to be ungovernable by at least a hundred political scientists per annum, but there has never been a shortage of candidates for the presidency. No candidate, however, plans to be a bad president; each hopes to be a superior one, a statesman.

We may safely conclude that it is nobler to be a statesman than a politician. By the same token, it is far better to be a statesman than a bureaucrat, for if the latter wishes to improve both his own lot and that of his country he will try to advance ever higher in the civil service. If he succeeds, however, his job will become ever more political. The bureaucrat's road to distinction leads through politics to statesmanship.

Statesmanship is not as rare as statesmen, because on occasion quite ordinary men are capable of the extraordinary deeds we designate as acts of statesmanship, but it is rare enough. This calls for comment only because statesmanship is presumed to be an art, and an art is traditionally understood as a teachable activity that can give an account of itself in terms of means and ends. For example, shoemaking is an art, and there are teachers of shoemaking who can teach novices to become shoemakers; it happens all the time. Unfortunately, the situation is different with regard to statesmanship. The true teachers of statesmen are not statesmen but political philosophers, and they are even harder to find than statesmen. For the most part we must rely on their books, but these yield their teachings reluctantly, and no reliable substitute for them has ever been found. It is surely true that neither departments of political science nor schools of public affairs do much in the way of training statesmen.

Even if we enjoyed a plenitude of teachers, we would have to search assiduously for students who are potential statesmen. Nature grants to very few the requisite combination of gifts, such as intelligence and a bent for practical affairs. (And they are gifts—which is why we speak of statesmen as having "charisma"—because nature owes us nothing in this respect, nor, perhaps, in any other respect.) Even if there were enough teachers of statesmanship and enough young men and women capable of being taught, we would still not be assured of enough statesmen. Fledgling statesmen must be in positions of authority to realize their potential, after all, and it is chance, as often as not, that decides who rules.

It is, then, impossible to systematize the production of statesmanship. The existence of a single statesman depends on the fortunate occurrence of a successful collaboration among teachers, students, and circumstance. The absence of statesmanship thus calls for no explanation, for it represents the normal, or at any rate the usual, state of affairs. We should remember as much when we are tempted to blame bureaucracy for precluding statesmanship.

### Historical Views of Statesmanship

Statesmanship is both a lofty and a rare phenomenon, but it is not lofty because of its rareness. If our country were suddenly to be graced by a dozen statesmen, it would not mean that statesmanship had been cheapened but only that we were, suddenly, a very lucky nation once again.

Statesmanship has been considered so lofty that neither Calvin nor Luther hesitated to consider it a divine calling.[3] A statesman, in their view, takes his orders directly from God, which means that he is in many ways above the laws of men. He is sovereign on earth, for he is the deputy of the Sovereign of all sovereigns.

Luther and Calvin had a contemporary, one of the greatest teachers of statesmen, who played down—to put it mildly—the role of divine Sovereignty without in the least denigrating the art of statesmanship. Machiavelli taught men that at the heights of its splendor statesmanship involves the greatest difficulties; it is by surmounting them that statesmanship becomes visible in its purest form and earns its practitioners the glory that is their most coveted reward.

Machiavelli knew full well that states will not always be threatened by extraordinary difficulties. Their leaders would then be faced with neither the need nor the opportunity to exercise the highest skills. Such rulers do not engage his interest because they must possess only "ordinary industriousness" and not virtue. Accordingly, Machiavelli spends much more time discussing the triumphs of the detestable Roman Emperor Severus than of the esteemed Emperor Marcus Aurelius. The latter was a great philosopher (like Machiavelli), but he was also a hereditary prince and thus attained a greater

---

[3] For a typical statement of statesmanship as a divine calling and its relationship to human law, see Jean Calvin, *Institutes of the Christian Religion*, trans. Henry Beveridge (Grand Rapids, Mich.: Eerdmans, 1957), IV, xx.

117

reputation for his power to think than for his power to rule. The greatest virtue of statesmen, according to Machiavelli, is to *found* states, always a difficult endeavor, though the greatest statesman may indeed found states in which the need for statesmanship at its highest disappears.[4]

Twentieth-century America runs little risk of finding itself in circumstances that would be good for its citizens and bad for its politically ambitious young men: a stability such that its leaders could rule well though their abilities rose no higher than ordinary industriousness. Conceivably Switzerland might attain to such tranquility, but even Switzerland's ability to survive the absence of statesmanship depends on the presence of statesmanship in the United States.

Difficulty is thus of the very essence of statesmanship. It is not enough to show that bureaucracy is an obstacle to statesmanship. A statesman's vocation necessarily involves the surmounting of obstacles, and the obstacles the American statesman confronts today are many. He must help to protect us against states committed to our destruction while he strives to avoid war with them. He must try to restore our sense of a mission beyond mere survival while he protects the freedom of those who deny we have a mission. It is in this context that the threat bureaucracy may pose to statesmanship must be judged. It would have to be demonstrated that the inconveniences of bureaucracy are *insurmountable* to maintain that bureaucracy is what deprives us of statesmanship.

The greatest obstacle to statesmanship in liberal democracies is almost certainly the political philosophy informing them and the institutions it spawns. The philosophers of liberal democracy from Hobbes and Locke onward were all the spiritual descendants of Niccolo Machiavelli. Machiavelli can be understood as the father of modern republicanism, which tended to become democratic republicanism. A crucial part of the domestication of "Old Nick" to the point where the Devil's disciple could be transformed into humanity's benefactor involved the progressive downgrading of the role of rulers and the concurrent increase of emphasis on institutions and laws. For example, it is undoubtedly true that our Founding Fathers learned a great deal from John Locke, but it is equally true that we acknowledge our indebtedness to him more for his advocacy of freedom under law

---

[4] Machiavelli's view of hereditary princes is set forth in chapter 2 of *The Prince*, ed. and trans. Mark Musa (New York: St. Martin's Press, 1964); his assessment of Marcus Aurelius can be found in chapter 19; and his esteem of founders in chapter 6. My understanding of Machiavelli has been decisively influenced by Leo Strauss, *Thoughts on Machiavelli* (Glencoe, N.Y.: Free Press, 1958). I have learned a great deal about the intimate connection between difficulty and statesmanship from an unpublished lecture by Professor James H. Nichols, "Reflections on Statesmanship."

and safeguarding of natural rights than for his espousal of a sweeping and almost unlimited executive prerogative.[5]

It is not difficult to see why. The history of liberal political philosophy involves a shift away from a preponderant concern with virtue and toward a concern with freedom and equality. Every statesman poses a challenge to the equality and liberty cherished by liberal democracy. He threatens equality because statesmanship is, in a way, superiority incarnate. All men may be created equal, but a statesman must be, or seem, better than the people he rules. Moreover, in crucial instances he must go beyond the law and the liberties it enshrines. Democracies do well to be uneasy about the episodes in their histories when the law was transgressed, for even justified actions can set bad examples, though it would be futile to deny that the Louisiana Purchase, to name but one example, was not effected constitutionally.

Quite naturally, then, an adage gains currency to the effect that democracies must not only be saved *by* heroes but *from* them—and statesmen are heroes. A statesman has a giant's strength but also a propensity to use that strength tyrannically, and the fear of tyranny has determined much of liberalism's words and deeds. Liberalism's energies are directed both against Christian princes whose only constraint is God and against "Machiavellian" princes who in principle act without any constraints whatsoever.[6]

The problem of controlling rulers is considered soluble in liberal democracies because while people had never really wanted to be virtuous, they actually do want to be free and equal. The many will therefore work together to control the few, and they will do so by institutions. In the process of making virtue a secondary consideration and, as Lord Acton puts it, insisting that liberty "is itself the highest political end," liberalism shows a continuing preoccupation with questions of power and its abuse. Hobbes had provided the first sustained discussion of power in the history of political philosophy, and three centuries later Lord Acton provided liberalism with its most famous motto on the subject when he stated that "power tends to corrupt and absolute power corrupts absolutely."[7] Men tended to forget that powerlessness also corrupts, and that many men—Harry

---

[5] For Locke on prerogative, see *Second Treatise of Government* (Indianapolis: Bobbs-Merrill, 1952), sections 160 ff.

[6] A relevant discussion of liberalism's fight against tyranny can be found at the beginning of the most famous work by liberalism's last great philosopher. See John Stuart Mill, *On Liberty* (Newbrook, Ill.: Crofts, 1947).

[7] Lord Acton's statement on liberty can be found in *Essays on Freedom and Power*, ed. Gertrude Himmelfarb (New York: Meridian Books, 1955), p. 74. Hobbes analyzes power in chapter 10 of the first part of *Leviathan* (Indianapolis: Bobbs-Merrill, 1958). That work is also, to my knowledge, the first classic of political philosophy to contain the word "power" in its full title.

119

Truman among them—have been ennobled by power. If liberals remembered this at all, they remembered it as an unfortunate necessity. Friedrich Hayek, a disciple of Lord Acton, was to write: "We shall never prevent the abuse of power if we are not prepared to limit power in a way which occasionally may also prevent its use for desirable purposes."[8] Hayek understands liberalism as a system where bad men can do the least harm. In his most influential book, *The Road to Serfdom*, he never discusses whether liberalism is not, by the same token, the system in which good men, especially statesmen, can do the least good.

If we understand liberalism as devotion to liberal democracy, and define such devotion so loosely—as we should—that it includes the views of men to the left of Senator George McGovern and to the right of Senator Barry Goldwater, then almost all of us are liberals. In that case, however, perhaps we should look benignly on bureaucracy not in spite of its alleged threat to statesmanship but because of it.

Our own liberal democracy illustrates rather than contradicts most of the above generalizations. The Founding Fathers were surely statesmen, but their belief that "they had created a system of institutions and an arrangement of the passions and interests that would be durable and self-perpetuating" has led even one of the most understanding students of their views to attribute to them a "failure to make provision for men of their own kind to come after them." They were statesmen who looked for an "institutional solution" to the problems of government.[9]

In this spirit they produced the Constitution of the United States. Before a benign visitor from other lands learns to revere that document as it deserves, he must be forgiven if he thinks of the regime it establishes as a kind of Rube Goldberg contraption. Everything in it seems to check and balance everything else, and almost anybody in government seems to be able to impede almost everybody else. This is owing, of course, to the very complicated separation of powers, in itself an example of modern philosophy's concern with abuse of power. Moreover, the Constitution gives, or at least intends to

---

[8] Friedrich Hayek, *The Road to Serfdom* (Chicago: University of Chicago Press, 1944), p. 237. Hayek acknowledges his indebtedness to Acton on pp. 13, 70, 144, 183 and quotes liberalism's "most famous motto" on p. 134.

[9] Martin Diamond, "Democracy and *The Federalist*: A Reconsideration of the Framers' Intent," *American Political Science Review*, vol. 53 (March 1959), p. 68. I had one occasion to discuss some of my thoughts on statesmanship and bureaucracy with Martin Diamond before his untimely death. My understanding of *The Federalist* owes nearly everything to him. On Jefferson's "institutional solution," see Harvey Mansfield, "Thomas Jefferson," in *American Political Thought*, ed. Frisch and Stevens, p. 50.

give, preponderant power not to the president but to the legislative branch. One can guess as much from the briefest glance at the document, which devotes the first and by far the longest of its seven articles to Congress. One can verify that guess by consulting the most authoritative commentary on the Constitution, *The Federalist*. It is true, of course, that senators and representatives can be statesmen, but their statesmanship—whether individual or part of a wise collective act of Congress—is not of the highest possible kind. Thus there could be only a few Founding Fathers and only one "father of our country."

A glance at *The Federalist* confirms the view that the Founders intended to circumscribe statesmanship. For our purpose, the eleven papers devoted to the presidency (Congress is the subject of fifteen) are the most illuminating ones. Publius begins his discussion by assuring his readers that the president does not have "royal prerogatives," and he concludes with an assurance that the office is duly dependent on the people and duly responsible. The president's lack of resemblance to the king of Great Britain is stressed repeatedly. Publius does not deny, to be sure, but rather asserts, the desirability of an executive who in his own way will be strong. In fact, he takes pride in the "constant probability" that the office will be "filled by characters pre-eminent for ability and virtue."[10] The two strongest arguments for the strength of the president are, however, most instructive. First, the United States needs one man with the power to conduct foreign affairs, simply because legislative bodies are too cumbersome in their dealings with other nations. Second, the president must have certain powers to counterbalance the otherwise overwhelming strength of the legislative branch.

Anyone who is inclined simply to dismiss the wisdom of the Founding Fathers in circumscribing the possibilities of statesmanship should first ponder the fact that this nation has been able to survive a large number of bad presidents. The Founding Fathers deserve even more credit. The government they designed may discourage statesmanship, but it does not preclude it, as witnessed by, for example, Jefferson and Lincoln—although it is necessary to add that both put a strain on the Constitution.

Nevertheless, the Constitution has survived them and remains in tolerably good health after 200 years. How, then, has it managed to accommodate itself to the dangers as well as splendors of states-

---

[10] *The Federalist*, No. 68., ed. Clinton Rossiter (New York: Mentor Books, 1961), p. 414. Nos. 67–77 of *The Federalist* deal with the presidency; all are attributed to Alexander Hamilton.

manship? First, the importance of foreign relations has constantly increased, and with it the power of the presidency. Secondly, the president has always had a special and unique access to national public opinion. Finally, the Constitution is amazingly brief, and its brevity is inseparable from its flexibility. It is silent on so many things that it can be adapted to the imperatives of changing circumstances.

As times change, some of the institutions that were part of a system of countervailing powers declined in vigor. The power of the states, for instance, is as nothing compared with what it was 200 years ago. But the genius of the system has been to permit the growth of substitute countervailing powers. One of them is the two-party system, of which the Constitution says not one word. Might not another be bureaucracy, about which the Constitution is also silent? [11]

## Historical Views of Bureaucracy

At this point we must shift our primary emphasis from statesmanship to bureaucracy. In order to do justice to it we must first try to understand it, and in order to understand it we must begin by seeing it in the best possible light. The greatest treatise on the value of bureaucracy is Hegel's *Philosophy of Right* (1821). For Hegel, the world and state of civil servants (*Beamtenwelt, Beamtenstaat*) are rational, that is to say good. It has become customary to translate *Beamtenstaat* as "bureaucratic state," which does no harm so long as one realizes that Hegel's use of the term carries no pejorative implications and that he does not use *Bürokratie*, a word that had already crept into German by 1800.

To Hegel, civil servants constitute a crucial element in both civil society and the state, in both the private and public spheres of communal life; as a matter of fact, they provide the essential link between the particular interests of the former and the universal concerns of the latter. That is why they are introduced as the universal estate or class (*Stand*) of civil society, and that is why they must be free from the burdens of earning a living in ordinary ways. They are an elite group possessed of *esprit de corps*, but membership in that select estate is open to all who possess sufficient talent and education.

Civil servants include a host of men with special expertise, such as doctors and lawyers; but the skill of their highest stratum, "the

---

[11] This paragraph owes a good deal to Herbert J. Storing, "Political Parties and the Bureaucracy," in *Political Parties, U.S.A.*, ed. Robert A. Goldwin (Chicago: Rand McNally, 1964), pp. 137–158.

executive civil servants" and "higher advisory officials," consists of nothing less than managing the state itself. Though their power must be subject to certain checks and balances, they need few external constraints since by disposition, training, and ability they derive their satisfaction from performing their duties. The bureaucracy is the modern equivalent of the ancient aristocracy; it is both the guardian and the embodiment of virtue, the jewel in the crown of the rational state.

Hegel's ideal state is a constitutional monarchy, but the functions and powers of the monarch are mainly symbolic and ceremonial, which means that the bureaucrats are the real rulers. One might thus assume that they are statesmen, and they do indeed possess some of the virtues associated with statesmanship. Yet, he says, "genius" is not an "objective qualification of civil service." Moreover, if difficulty is of the essence of statesmanship, it is impossible for them to be statesmen of the highest rank because no difficult tasks remain for them to perform. They are the contented administrators of a smoothly functioning organic whole.

Hegel's term for great statesmen such as Alexander and Napoleon is "world-historical individuals." These are men whose mighty labors prepare for the rational state, but they are the instruments of the "cunning of reason" without themselves being rational. Now that the rational state is secure in its existence, they are a thing of the past. In a very real sense statesmanship has become a superfluous commodity because *"what is rational is actual and what is actual is rational."* [12]

An easily discernible connection exists between Hegel's views and those of the greatest twentieth-century student of bureaucracy, Max Weber; it has even been maintained that the former presents "a model of bureaucracy almost identical with the Weberian ideal type." [13]

Both Hegel and Weber associate the bureaucratic with the ra-

---

[12] I have used the T. M. Knox translation of Hegel's *Philosophy of Right* (London: Oxford University Press, 1952). My exposition follows Hegel's order and is based primarily on sections 202, 205, 207, 289–297, and 303 from which all quotations except those of the last paragraph are taken. For Hegel on world historical individuals, see his *Philosophy of History*, trans. J. Sibree (New York: Dover, 1956), pp. 29–40. The last quotation (emphasis in the original) is from the Preface of *Philosophy of Right*, p. 10. For the exposition of this section I owe more than I can acknowledge by specific citation to Pierre Hassner's chapter on Hegel in *History of Political Philosophy*, ed. Leo Strauss and Joseph Cropsey (Chicago: Rand McNally, 1972), pp. 686–712.

[13] Shlomo Avineri, *Hegel's Theory of the Modern State* (Cambridge: Cambridge University Press, 1972), p. 160.

tional. Weber's voluminous writings on the subject abound with statements to that effect.[14] Thus bureaucracy depends and thrives on the elimination of all "irrational and emotional elements which escape calculation. This is the specific nature of bureaucracy and it is appraised as its special virtue." Bureaucracy is the means for turning the deeds of a community into "rationally ordered" social action. It tends naturally to promote a "rational . . . structure of domination."

Such examples could be multiplied almost at will, but they would conceal the vast differences between Hegel and Weber. To the former, bureaucracy derives both its rationality and its value from its service to a good end, the public interest. Moreover, the Hegelian state is part of an even grander rationality, a cosmos. Where Hegel finds rational order, Weber discerns only chaos, or at most a reality the meaning of which reason is unable to decipher. In other words, for Weber rationality is something entirely instrumental, in the service of ends it is incompetent to judge. Ultimately, Weber can mean no more by "being rational" than "being efficient and proficient"; bureaucracy is rational only because of its "technical superiority over any other form of organization."

Given this state of affairs, however, rationality has nothing to recommend it over irrationality. In his devotion, even to the point of obsession, to a value-free social science, Weber attempts to describe bureaucracy without condoning or condemning it, but his description unmistakably conveys a distaste for it. The rationalized world is equated with stultification and disenchantment, and who would not rather be enchanted? The question then becomes whether anything can be done about modern bureaucracy.

Rejecting the determinism of Marx and embracing the vitalism of Nietzsche, Weber held fast to the possibility of political and social renewal by means of statesmanship. His name for it was "charismatic authority," a concept that obviates the need and conceals the inability to distinguish between statesmen and tyrants, for both Churchill and Hitler were endowed with charisma.

Weber postulates a complex and dialectical relationship between bureaucracy and statesmanship. On the one hand, bureaucracy tends

---

[14] All the quotations from Weber can be found in *From Max Weber: Essays in Sociology*, trans. and ed. H. H. Gerth and C. Wright Mills (New York: Oxford University Press, 1946). See the section on bureaucracy (pp. 196–244) and charismatic authority (pp. 245–252); see especially pp. 103, 216, 228, and 240. The most succinct statement of Weber's on the scope and limits of reason is "Science as a Vocation," pp. 129–156. An authoritative discussion of Weber and Marx can be found in Karl Löwith, *Gesammelte Abhandlungen* (Stuttgart: Kohlhammer Verlag, 1960), pp.1–67. Weber's connection with Nietzsche is explored by William Shapiro, "The Nietzschean Roots of Max Weber's Social Science," unpublished Ph.D. dissertation, Cornell University, 1978.

forever to petrify the statesman's work by routinizing it, but on the other hand bureaucracies tend to be remarkably docile when confronted by a strong will. What is more, while bureaucratization has an innate tendency to spread, this expansion is not necessarily synonymous with the expansion of its power. Bureaucratic and charismatic domination "do not stand opposed, with no connections or transition between them."[15] Relief is always temporary but always possible.

## Bureaucracy Today

When we consider bureaucracy in this country today, we notice above all the great amount of talk about the subject. Though the word "bureaucracy" is on many lips, in bars as well as in universities, it is used to mean a number of related but different things, and some clarification is needed.

> The first and the most traditional usage corresponds to a concept of political science: bureaucracy is government by bureaus. In other words, it is government by departments of the state staffed by appointed and not elected functionaries, organized hierarchically, and dependent on a sovereign authority. Bureaucratic power, in this sense, implies the reign of law and order, but, at the same time, government without the participation of the governed. The second usage originates with Max Weber and has been propagated especially by sociologists and historians: bureaucratization is the rationalization of collective activities. This bureaucratization is brought about by, among other means, the inordinate concentration of the units of production and in general of all organizations and the development within these of a system of impersonal rules, as much for the definition of functions and the repartition of responsibilities as for the ordering of careers. The third usage corresponds to the vulgar and frequent sense of the word "bureaucracy." It evokes the slowness, the ponderousness, the routine, the complication of procedures, and the maladapted responses of "bureaucratic" organizations to the needs which they should satisfy, and the frustrations which their members, clients or subjects consequently endure.[16]

Let us not shun the "vulgar and frequent" sense of the word,

---

[15] *From Max Weber*, p. 426. Weber is here referring primarily, but by no means exclusively, to conditions in ancient China.
[16] Michael Crozier, *The Bureaucratic Phenomenon* (Chicago: University of Chicago Press, 1964), p. 3.

for it is above all in that sense that the word impinges on our consciousness in a democratic country, and it is because of the things to which that word points that we find bureaucracy repulsive. We stand in too many lines at the post office; fill out too many incomprehensible forms; wait too long for public services; brook too much interference from Washington in the way we run our businesses, make, buy, and sell our goods, teach our classes, live our lives.

Because of these kinds of intrusions, bureaucracy has become a leading political issue. We have become accustomed to seeing it as an issue the right uses against the left. We are not surprised when Governor Reagan berates bureaucracy, but when Governor Brown does we begin to wonder whether the "new politics" is not making way for a "new, new politics."[17]

In other words, we have come to see bureaucracy as primarily a left-wing phenomenon, a view that is only partly convincing. It is undeniable that one of the afflictions Communist and even Socialist countries have to bear is excessive bureaucratization; it is no less true that Nazi Germany was a most bureaucratic country. Adolf Eichmann issued his orders from Bureau IV-B-4 of the RSHA. When Hitler took office, according to Speer, "the old bureaucratic apparatus continued to run the affairs of state smoothly. . . ."[18] He soon developed an intense prejudice against that old apparatus because it was frustrating his plans—could that bureaucracy have been all bad?—but he simply replaced it with a new one of which Speer was part. In the end Speer blames the bureaucracy for his ignorance of what was going on in the death camps—though he had visited them.

If we simple-mindedly label bureaucracy a left-wing phenomenon in the United States, we must explain away a number of facts. One is that the most powerful American bureaucrat of this century was J. Edgar Hoover. The most recalcitrant bureaucratic sovereignty has traditionally been considered to reside in the State Department. When conservatives rail against bureaucracy at HEW, they forfeit some credibility by failing to rail against the bureaucracy of the Pentagon. The target of their wrath may understandably be some of the policies of HEW, but does this not amount to an admission on their part that bureaucracy per se is not the primary obstacle to good government?

---

[17] On the "new, new politics," see a perceptive article under that title by Marc F. Plattner in *The Alternative*, vol. 10, no. 10 (August-September 1977), pp. 22–24.
[18] See Albert Speer, *Inside the Third Reich* (New York: Avon, 1971), p. 56. See also pp. 68, 103, 273, 286, 652–658. Details about Eichmann and "his" office can be found in Lucy S. Dawidowicz, *The War against the Jews* (New York: Avon, 1976), pp. 132–141, 154.

Many honorable opponents of bureaucracy hate and fear it because they see it as a threat to capitalism. The United States is and was designed to be a commercial republic; they fear that bureaucratic interference threatens the free enterprise system that has made our wealth and freedom the envy of the world. That argument must be confronted with the utmost seriousness, for it contains a good deal of the truth—which is also to say that it does not contain the whole truth.

It is worth remembering that Weber saw an affinity between bureaucracy and capitalism; he writes at length of "the bureaucratic organizations of private capitalism."[19] His argument is far from conclusive for at least two reasons. First, Weber tends to use the terms "capitalism," "industrial capitalism," and "industrialism" interchangeably. Second, had he had more time to study the emerging Socialist and Communist regimes of our century, he might well have come to the conclusion that Socialism would only increase bureaucratization; and one can in fact find many remarks of his to that effect.

Nevertheless, the bureaucratization of American capitalism deserves notice. The typical feature of American capitalism is not the corner grocery store but the corporation, and corporations suffer from a vast number of bureaucratic afflictions. If one concedes that their first objective is, and perhaps ought to be, the making of profits, one must concede that they may work against the common good. In that case private bureaucracies will have to be controlled by agencies that are bound to turn into public bureaucracies.

Most of the arguments attempting to prove that private bureaucracy is preferable to public bureaucracy fail to carry full conviction. Let us briefly examine three of them.

First, we are told that private bureaucracies compete against each other to the public's advantage. But public bureaucracies also compete against each other, possibly to the public's advantage. Any observer of the Washington scene—or attentive student of the *United States Government Manual*—knows that government bureaucracy is not nearly so monolithic a phenomenon as polemics against it make it out to be.

Second, we are told that private enterprise is more efficient than any government business. The record makes this impossible to deny in many cases, but one must add that many a private corporation is not nearly so tightly organized as the more extreme advocates of free enterprise would like to think. Anyone who has worked for a large

---

[19] *From Max Weber*, pp. 202–204, 214–216, 228.

firm will know that many of its employees have developed the ability to do as little work as possible into a fine art.

Private bureaucracies are also held to be less dangerous because their excesses are more easily visible and held to account. Officials of corporations are constantly fired because of profit-and-loss considerations, while government bureaucrats are often impossible to fire. Yet a great deal of inefficiency within a corporation is compatible with a great deal of corporate profit. It is true that when corporations lose money, heads roll in the top echelons of executives; but when government agencies fail to perform their functions, the top echelons, not usually protected by civil service regulations, can also be called to account. It is a myth that J. Edgar Hoover could not have been fired. If President Truman could discharge General MacArthur, he or any of his successors could have dismissed Hoover. Such action would certainly have required courage, but statesmanship *always* requires courage. Similarly, it is a myth to say that government bureaucrats are "immune to pressure." They are, rather, "sitting ducks" to the pressures of public opinion, the usual source of the convictions informing their actions.

The pervasiveness of the bureaucratic phenomenon leads to questions we are unable either to avoid or settle. Is bureaucracy really a self-perpetuating and inevitable phenomenon? When we worry about it and its deleterious effects might we not be worrying about an inevitable by-product of more fundamental problems of government, such as bigness, technology, and industrialism?

These questions are not meant to be rhetorical, but rather unanswerable—at least by this writer. Let us suppose for a moment, however, that bureaucracy *is* merely a symptom of bigness, technology, and industrialism. In that case we can and ought to do much less about it than we might like. We can hardly become a small country, because the Constitution necessarily implies an extended republic. We can hardly surrender our technological sophistication because of the imperatives of national security. We can hardly become less industrial, because our material well-being depends on our vast productivity. We could still fight to contain bureaucracy, but we might have to view it as one of those minor curses that usually come with major blessings.[20]

## The Reciprocal Influence of Statesmanship and Bureaucracy

We conclude these observations by reflecting on statesmanship and bureaucracy in today's—and tomorrow's—United States and by re-

---

[20] On the "extended republic," see *Federalist*, No. 10, pp. 82–84.

minding the reader that the author's purpose has been to raise doubts that bureaucracy is a primary cause of our lack of statesmen and statesmanship.

Because an adversary relationship between statesmen and bureaucrats is too often taken for granted, it is important to mention that a president may very well need, use, and depend on bureaucracy. For example, an ecological disaster might conceivably threaten the country (in spite of the foolishness of much of the rhetoric of so many of our fanatical ecologists); it is possible to imagine, say, a dire shortage of wood and an epidemic of rare diseases destroying our forests. A statesman need not be able to tell a sycamore from a pine, but he must have the counsel of people who can. In such a case the president would rely heavily on the special expertise of the Department of Agriculture's Forest Service, a bureaucratic agency without known and fatal blemishes.

The above example may not be a good one for a variety of reasons—one of them being that everyone, as it were, loves a forest ranger. Let us, therefore, turn to the State Department, since almost no one, as it were, loves "those guys in striped pants." Moreover, the State Department has been judged by many as overly bureaucratic and given to subverting the will of the president as well as the public.

In studying bureaucracy in the State Department we are in the happy position of being able to draw on the insights of Henry A. Kissinger. Writing in 1966, Kissinger characterized the leadership of the United States and other liberal democracies as "bureaucratic-pragmatic," especially in regard to foreign policy. Excessive attention to "technical issues" was particularly detrimental to the conduct of international relations. "In the bureaucratic societies policy emerges from a compromise which often produces the least common denominator, and it is implemented by individuals whose reputation is made by administering the status quo."[21]

The obvious difficulty of Professor Kissinger's scheme of classification is that it does not explain Secretary of State Kissinger. He was neither a lawyer nor a businessman by training; he did not make his reputation by administering the status quo; and the man who became known as the "Lone Ranger" was certainly not crippled by bureaucratic entanglements.

In the case of his superior, the issue is more complicated. President Nixon tangled with the federal bureaucracy and did not emerge as victor. Theodore H. White writes:

---

[21] Henry A. Kissinger, "Domestic Structure and Foreign Policy," *Daedalus*, vol. 95, no. 2 (Spring 1966), p. 524. Later published in his *American Foreign Policy* (New York: Norton, 1969), pp. 11–50. See especially p. 43.

all Presidents are appalled by the sluggishness of the millions of men and women who turn the wheels of government—or who slow those wheels when the President attempts to speed them up, or who cling to the familiar out of inertia when a President wants to change. To this permanent affliction of all Presidents was added the real condition that the Federal bureaucracy for forty years, with the single interruption of the benign administration of Dwight D. Eisenhower, has been staffed by Democrats, and its leaders promoted by Democrats.[22]

After Nixon's fall one of his aides could attribute the catastrophe to his having had to operate in "a totally hostile environment." He specified bureaucracy as part of that environment, but also the press and Congress.

One of Nixon's legitimate grievances against the bureaucracy was its leaking of government secrets; a bureaucrat named Ellsberg publicized what came to be known as the Pentagon Papers. The President, however, might have turned that deplorable incident to his advantage by using the leaked material to prove that our Vietnam involvement was a mess that was by no stretch of the imagination his own making.

Instead, Nixon resolved to "get" the bureaucracy—or, to put it more justly, to work on the reorganization of government. It was to be one of the major tasks of his second term in office. It scarcely needs saying that the bureaucracy reacted gracelessly, deviously, and viciously, but it will not do to say that the bureaucracy caused the fall of Richard Nixon. It could administer punishing blows to him, because he was always a vulnerable president whose support was never deep even when it was wide. It could leak ghastly stories about him, but he provided an amazing number of ghastly stories to leak. It could frustrate his will, but in a not inconsiderable number of cases it was thereby performing a public service.

Before his fall President Nixon exercised great power, even as his predecessors in office had done, so that talk of an "imperial presidency" became current. One notes that alarm about the power of the president grows apace with alarm about the power of the bureaucracy. Is that not a potent argument in favor of the compatibility of statesmanship and bureaucracy? One could, of course, contend that neither Kissinger nor Nixon was a statesman, and go on to reason that bureaucracy is so diabolical that it permits the bad and prohibits the good use of power, but this is a line of reasoning that would have to be seen to be disbelieved.

---

[22] Theodore H. White, *Breach of Faith* (New York: Dell, 1976), pp. 153–154; see also pp. 156, 188–190, and 225.

A much more serious concern is that whereas bureaucracy can accommodate itself to statesmen, it is ultimately fatal to democracy. On the face of it nothing seems more obvious than that rule of the experts is incompatible with the rule of the many. Weber devoted a considerable amount of attention to this problem. He thought that in some ways bureaucracy is itself an instrument of democratization, because it frequently supplants a governing aristocracy and because the impersonal rule of law it imposes has a leveling effect. Moreover, democracy is frequently the fertile soil for bureaucratization. But many things that grow in the soil are not good for the soil. To be more specific: Weber saw no great hope for parliaments. He could envision a future for plebiscitarian democracy, but ours is representative democracy.[23]

If Weber is right, bureaucracy may pose the greatest danger to congressional statesmanship rather than to the wise use of presidential power; but is Weber right? The proliferation of administrative law lends a certain plausibility to his views, but Congress is far from being on the road to impotence. Administrative law flourishes in part because, to revert to an earlier example, members of Congress need know as little about trees as presidents do, but in part also because Congress has been careless in delegating its powers. Sufficient care will admittedly not solve the whole problem, but Congress can do other good things than pass laws. (As a matter of fact, it passes too many laws anyway.) It can check the excesses of bureaucracy by becoming a more imposing forum for the voicing of opinions a bureaucracy is bound to heed—not the transitory views measured by public opinion polls, but the basic convictions to which a democratic citizenry and a bureaucracy devoted to its service must subscribe. Congress has an educational function, one that grows more urgent as it becomes apparent that universities are failing in their appointed tasks and thus trailing off into the marginal position they deserve.

It is in the educating and shaping of a true public opinion that Congress and the president can cooperate to thwart the dangers bureaucracy poses. Bureaucracy is often a kind of illness, but it is not a terminal disease. Let anyone who thinks it is look to Israel, a country burdened by far greater bureaucratization than ours. It remains in decisive respects a healthy nation, nevertheless, because of both its firm resolve to survive and its faithfulness, under incredible pressures, to the principles that gave it birth.

The two greatest difficulties to which any president of the United States must address himself are the threat from hostile nations abroad and a lack of clarity, as well as fervor, about our basic principles at

---

[23] See *From Max Weber*, pp. 103 ff., 209, 224 ff.

home. Put in other terms, it may very well be the case that our leading domestic problem is the alleged or real death of God, and the overwhelming sense of meaninglessness attending it. Nothing will be gained and a great deal can be lost by magnifying the bureaucratic problem out of all proportion. The president has enough to do already in protecting us from communism and nihilism.

One suspects that in invigorating the nation the president may have to be more demagogic at times than suits our taste, but fortunately for us excessive fastidiousness is not a common characteristic of statesmen. His work will certainly not be easy, but only philosophers and scholars are pledged to look at even terrible truths unflinchingly. A statesman is permitted to hold fast to a nourishing illusion, as did Disraeli in his "long youthfulness of heart" when he cherished the motto *Forti nihil difficile*—to the brave nothing is difficult.[24]

---

[24] See André Maurois, *Disraeli* (New York: Modern Library, 1928), pp. 236, 365.

# Contributors

EDWARD C. BANFIELD is the George D. Markham Professor of Government, Harvard University. His books include *The Unheavenly City Revisited, Big City Politics, Political Influence,* and *The Moral Basis of a Backward Society.*

WERNER J. DANNHAUSER is professor of government, Cornell University. He is the author of *Nietzsche's View of Socrates* and articles and reviews in *Commentary, American Scholar, National Review,* the *American Political Science Review,* and other magazines and professional journals. From 1964 to 1968 he was associate editor of *Commentary.*

MICHAEL J. MALBIN is a resident fellow at the American Enterprise Institute, a contributing editor to *National Journal,* and adjunct associate professor of politics at Catholic University. He is the author of *Religion and Politics* and *Unelected Representatives: The New Role of Congressional Staff* and the editor of *Parties, Interest Groups, and Campaign Finance Laws.*

MARK H. MOORE is associate professor of public policy, John F. Kennedy School of Government, Harvard University. He has served as special assistant to the administrator and chief planning officer in the Drug Enforcement Administration of the U. S. Department of Justice. While a consultant to the Hudson Institute, he wrote the third volume of *The Economics of Heroin Distribution.*

GUSTAVE H. SHUBERT is senior vice-president of the Rand Corporation and heads the corporation's Domestic Programs Division. He is a trustee of the New York City–Rand Institute and served as its president in 1971–1972.

LAURENCE H. SILBERMAN is executive vice-president for government relations, Crocker National Bank. He has served as under secretary of labor, as deputy attorney general, and as ambassador to Yugoslavia.

HERBERT J. STORING was, at the time of his death in 1977, the Robert Kent Gooch Professor of Government and director of the Program on the Presidency of the White Burkett Miller Center for Public Affairs, University of Virginia. He was the author of *The Complete Anti-Federalist* and *Black American Political Thought* and the editor of *What Country Have I? Political Writings by Black Americans* and *Essays on the Scientific Study of Politics.*

# SELECTED AEI PUBLICATIONS

*Public Opinion,* published bimonthly (one year, $12; two years, $22; single copy, $2.50)

*A Conversation with Gerald R. Ford: Thoughts on Economics and Politics in the 1980s* (19 pp., $2.25)

*A Conversation with George Bush* (26 pp., $3.25)

*Choosing Presidential Candidates: How Good Is the New Way?* John Charles Daly, mod. (30 pp., $3.75)

*The Changing British Party System, 1945-1979,* S.E. Finer (264 pp., $7.25)

*A Conversation with Philip M. Crane* (25 pp., $2.25)

*A Conversation with Vladimir Bukovsky* (22 pp., $2.25)

*The Denigration of Capitalism: Six Points of View,* Michael Novak, ed. (64 pp., $4.25).

*Church, State and Public Policy: The New Shape of the Church-State Debate,* Jay Mechling, ed. (119 pp., paper $5.25, cloth $10.25)

*A Conversation with Mayor Marion Barry* (18 pp., $2.25)

*A Conversation with Anne de Lattre: Developing the Sahel* (19 pp., $2.25)

*A Conversation with Ernesto Mulato: The Political and Military Struggle in Angola* (23 pp., $2.25)

*Prices subject to change without notice.*

# AEI ASSOCIATES PROGRAM

The American Enterprise Institute invites your participation in the competition of ideas through its AEI Associates Program. This program has two objectives:

The first is to broaden the distribution of AEI studies, conferences, forums, and reviews, and thereby to extend public familiarity with the issues. AEI Associates receive regular information on AEI research and programs, and they can order publications and cassettes at a savings.

The second objective is to increase the research activity of the American Enterprise Institute and the dissemination of its published materials to policy makers, the academic community, journalists, and others who help shape public attitudes. Your contribution, which in most cases is partly tax deductible, will help ensure that decision makers have the benefit of scholarly research on the practical options to be considered before programs are formulated. The issues studied by AEI include:

- Defense Policy
- Economic Policy
- Energy Policy
- Foreign Policy
- Government Regulation
- Health Policy
- Legal Policy
- Political and Social Processes
- Social Security and Retirement Policy
- Tax Policy

For more information, write to:

AMERICAN ENTERPRISE INSTITUTE
1150 Seventeenth Street, N.W.
Washington, D.C. 20036